Thy Will Be Done

A Guide to Wills, Taxation, and
Estate Planning for Older Persons

Eugene J. Daly, Attorney at Law

Golden Age Books

Prometheus Books
AMHERST, NEW YORK

Published 1994 by Prometheus Books
59 John Glenn Drive, Amherst, New York 14228-2197

This publication is designed to provide accurate and authoritative information in regard to the subject matter covered. It is sold with the understanding that the author and the publisher are not engaged in rendering legal, accounting, or other professional service. If legal advice or other expert assistance is required, the individual and personal service of a competent professional person should be sought. (From a Declaration of Principles jointly adopted by a Committee of the American Bar Association and a Committee of Publishers.)

Library of Congress Cataloging-in-Publication Data

Daly, Eugene J.
    Thy will be done : a guide to wills, taxation, and estate planning for older persons / by Eugene J. Daly.
        p.   cm. — (Golden age books)
    ISBN 0-87975-903-8 (pbk. : acid-free paper)
    1. Wills—United States—Popular works. 2. Trusts and trustees—United States—Popular works. 3. Estate planning—United States—Popular works. 4. Inheritance and transfer tax—Law and legislation—United States—Popular works. 5. Aged—Legal status, laws, etc.—United States—Popular works. I. Title. II. Series.
KF755.Z9D35   1994
346.7305′4—dc20
[347.30654]
                                                                                        94-4962
                                                                                        CIP

Printed on acid-free paper in the United States of America

I dedicate this book to those who survived the Depression and who went on to display the most dedicated work ethic of any generation. Although this book gives you information about what happens to your assets after your death, it also offers information about life. It will save you money and, hopefully, it will make life easier for you and your survivors.

Contents

PART TWO: AFTER DEATH

PART THREE: TAXATION

Preface to the Second Edition

Since the initial publication of *Thy Will Be Done,* not much has changed regarding wills, taxation, and estate planning for older persons. People continue to procrastinate, while the great majority die without preparing a last will and testament. It seems that people still harbor extreme feelings about lawyers, who are either loved or hated.

Thankfully, more and more people are coming to accept the value of making a will. I hope this awareness impresses upon them the equally important need for planning their estates. The very best of intentions can be in vain if a plan to protect valuable assets has not been put in place.

For those of you who are concerned about the Revenue Reconciliation Act of 1993 (President Clinton's tax law), I have some good news: the changes are not too dramatic. As you probably know, the major change is an increase in the tax rates. However, it is still the case that no federal estate tax is assessed on taxable estates valued at less than $600,000.

Because this volume is not a "how to do it yourself" book (but more about "how to understand your lawyer"), Prometheus Books and I have decided to republish it in the hope that more of you will heed the call to take charge of your property and your assets by committing your final wishes to the safety of a will that is combined with thoughtful and money-saving estate planning.

So, read on, think about your will, see your attorney, plan your estate, and . . . thy will be done.

E.J.D.

Preface to the First Edition

The purpose of this book is to familiarize you and your advisors—perhaps even your children—with a *will, estate administration,* and *estate taxation.* It explains how a variety of laws affect you or someone close to you.

These subjects are discussed in clear terms: I avoid using technical language except where absolutely necessary. This book is the product of fourteen years of legal practice during which I listened to questions posed by average people—like you—some of whom had a net worth of five hundred dollars, while that of others exceeded a few hundred thousand. In these pages you will become acquainted with their questions and my answers.

Other books have been written on this subject. They describe how to write your will and how to administer an estate without an attorney's advice. Many contain charts and forms and suggestions for readers who want to avoid an attorney's fee. What I offer is general information; whether you choose to seek the services of an attorney is your decision. It is my opinion, however, that you should not consider my summary of ideas as a substitute for the advice of your own attorney. Laws are technical, they vary from state to state, and they change from time to time.

This book teaches you how to talk to your attorney, your family, and anyone else who might be helping you with your finances or with the many other concerns that older people confront. It also teaches children and caregivers how to advise their elder parents or clients.

You will learn what happens to your possessions after your death, how a will allows you to determine who will receive those possessions, and the extent of your power to appoint the person who will supervise your estate after you are gone. You will also learn about the work that has to be performed by those who are chosen to supervise an estate.

In addition, as a result of my discussion of the living will, you will learn what choices you have regarding a dignified death. Also, you will learn what taxes your estate must pay.

How will you learn all of these things? By reading about the successes and misfortunes of others. I have analyzed the experiences of many clients, and will share these experiences with you.

May this book enrich your life, not only by saving you money, but by helping you solve a few worrisome problems.

Acknowledgments

Writing this book would have been impossible if not for the constant patience and encouragement of my dear wife, Joan. Thank you so much.

However, near the end of the project, I became acutely aware of the closeness of my readers. Knowing these wise and kind people gave my confidence a boost: my friends Philip J. Trabulsy, Jr., and Patrick A. Naughton, who have helped me to believe in my legal ability; the maternal optimist Lillian E. McGowan, who convinced me not to abandon this book; the philanthropic fundraiser Eileen F. Smith, who has consistently asked me to address her audiences of potential donors; and attorneys Richard B. Covey, William R. Dunlop, and Evan R. Dawson, who offered suggestions on how a general audience book on technical subjects balances accuracy and readability. To them, my sincerest gratitude.

My thanks to Steven L. Mitchell, editor of the Golden Age Books series for Prometheus; he personally edited and enthusiastically published my first book. The tireless assistance of my associates, Teri Lombardi and, especially, Elaine Dolan, is also much appreciated.

I want to mention my recently departed legal mentors, Edward M. and Esther K. Benton. They shared with me what they learned in their combined total of almost 120 years of writing wills and administering estates. I miss their friendship and, particularly, their Friday night open house.

To my clients over the years, thank you for telling me, teaching me, and trusting me. To you I offer this book in tribute.

Part One

Preparing Your Will

1

Introduction

DYING WITHOUT A WILL

Dying without a will is known as *dying intestate*. If you die without a will, the state does not take your property. Instead, it will go to your next of kin, what attorneys call your *distributees* or *heirs-at-law*. Each state has its own law defining the next of kin, but here are some general guidelines, typical of the law in most states, to help you identify these persons.

If you are survived by a *spouse* (and not survived by a child or parent), your spouse receives all your property.

If you are survived by *a spouse and a parent* (and not survived by a child), your spouse and your parent share your property.

If you are survived by *a spouse, a child, and a parent,* your spouse and your child share your property, and your parent receives nothing.

If you are *not* survived by *a spouse or a child or a parent,* your brothers and sisters, and the children of your deceased brothers and sisters, share your property.

If you do not desire your property to be distributed to those who would receive it if you were to die intestate, *have a will prepared.* Perhaps you are hesitant to execute a will because of one or more of the following mistaken ideas:

a superstition that if you draw up a will, you are *soon to die;*

an expectation of paying an *exorbitant attorney's fee;*

a theory that if you die after having made a will, a court will *entangle your finances;*

a misconception that if a will exists, the *estate tax will be increased;*

a fear that if you name someone in your will to receive your possessions, *you will not really remain the owner;*

an "I don't" attitude: "I don't have anything to leave anyone"; "I don't have any family or friends"; "I don't care if they fight over my possessions" (a variation of "I don't believe my children will have any problem dividing my possessions"); "I don't worry about it because I will be gone." It is this last depressing "I don't" proclamation that is most frequently heard.

Many people die without a will. But it is within *your* power to determine who receives *your* assets. My goal, which I hope to achieve, is to convince you to have a will.

Sample Situation

Mary and her sister Margaret have lived together and have shared their lives and fortunes. They worked hard and saved their money. Although they consider themselves poor, they have accumulated a substantial amount of money. Their parents are dead, neither sister has married, and neither has had a child. They do have a brother, Charlie, whom neither sister has seen since he ventured off at age sixteen to seek his fortune. When Mary or Margaret dies, the surviving sister and Charlie will split the deceased sister's estate if there is no will. *Charlie will then have found his fortune.*

Executing a will prevents this unfortunate distribution of the deceased sister's estate. Each sister has the right to direct that her sister is to receive everything, and her brother is to receive nothing. Another situation requiring a will, though perhaps not as dramatic but still significant, is your right to choose the recipient of an heirloom or any other possession you might own. Perhaps Margaret *does want* Charlie to receive a particular item. If so, it should be so stated in Margaret's will. *Each of us has the right to select those who are to receive our property.* Do not let the law make this decision for you; do not die without a will.

Money-Saving Suggestions

When your will is prepared, you benefit as well as the survivors who in-herit your possessions. The preparation of a will is an ideal time to review your investments, *a time to learn something about your financial health.* Often changes in investment strategies result. I call this the *living motive* for a will.

In addition to reviewing existing investments, preparing a will provides the perfect opportunity to inventory your possessions: a list of all bank accounts, including Individual Retirement Accounts (IRAs) and certificates of deposit (CDs); employee benefits; stock certificates; and any debts owed *to* you. The location of your *safe deposit box* (if you have one) should definitely be included in your inventory. If you own a home, a copy of the *deed* should be inventoried, along with deeds to other real estate holdings, including your cemetery plot.

There are two reasons for reviewing and inventorying your assets. When you die, your inventory will make it easy for your heirs to locate these assets. But more importantly, you now have *greater control* over your possessions because you have an *orderly record* and a *sharper under-standing* of what you own.

When your will is prepared, you might also want to consider talking with your attorney about a "living will." Age brings a variety of health concerns, including the fear that a medical emergency or a prolonged illness could arise in which a decision would have to be made regarding life-saving or life-sustaining measures. The living will (about which more will be said in chapter 8) would outline your wishes. Though older persons are more likely to concern themselves with such an eventuality, the living will is a document to consider no matter how old you are. Accidents and medical tragedies know no age boundaries.

WHY HAVE A WILL?

Your ownership of property exists not only during your lifetime, but also after your death. Your will is your hand from the grave, so to speak, a hand that conducts the distribution of your property. A person who makes a will is called a *testator*. Why is it better to be a testator than to die intestate?

You select who will receive your property (called your *estate*) after your death.

You determine whether your estate is left in a *trust,* and you will learn how this gives the designated recipient the benefit of the money, but denies the recipient the control of the money.

You select the person or bank (called an *executor*) who will supervise your estate.

You leave money to your favorite *charity.*

You select who will receive your furniture, clothing, jewelry, and other *personal effects.*

You select who will *enforce any legal rights* that you may have had at the time of your death.

You plan your estate so there will be a *minimum of tax.*

You give advice on your *burial wishes* (but be sure to tell a close relative or friend about your burial preference).

As I mentioned above, you have a will for what I call the *living motive* —it is a time to review your assets and to organize your financial life.

I offer a word of caution. Do not use a will to hurt someone, or to have the last nasty word. The person will never hear it, *because only on television and in the movies is there a reading of the will.* In the real world, people learn about being named in a will when the attorney for the deceased person's executor notifies them of their good fortune.

Sample Situation

John says that his mother, Gladys, does not need a will; she is not *rich* and her financial affairs are *simple.* What John's mother *should have* is a *simple will.* Though she may not be rich, she's probably not poor either. In all likelihood, her financial affairs are not so simple.

Many people *underestimate* their net worth and the net worth of others. They *overestimate* their ability to handle money, as well as the ability of others to handle financial matters. For many older people the denial of wealth avoids *guilt,* and the denial of financial confusion avoids an *admission of inadequacy.* These defenses lead to the unfortunate conclusion that a will is not necessary, either for yourself or for someone you love.

If Gladys is one of the many people who die without a will, the law determines who receives her property and who is appointed to supervise the distribution of that property. Perhaps the people who receive her property, if she dies intestate, are not the people Gladys would have chosen; perhaps the person appointed to supervise the distribution of her property is not the person she would have chosen. Our system allows individuals to own property, and control its destination after the owner's death. *You cannot take it with you.* So exercise your right to choose who receives what you leave behind, and who is to represent your estate. *You should have a will, and you should suggest that those you love consider making a will as well.*

Money-Saving Suggestions

It is false to say that only a millionaire needs a will. Those who are not so rich also need a will to select the people who are to receive whatever property is owned at the time of death. Don't be put off by rumors that wills cost a lot to prepare. Having a will drawn up should not be expensive (anywhere from one hundred to a few hundred dollars, depending on its extent and complexity). I suggest you have a will so that *your survivors will save time and energy after your death since your affairs will then be in order.*

As for the more well off among us, it is through a will that tax-saving techniques are implemented. In Part Three, I will analyze these techniques and demonstrate how "trusts" can save *estate taxes.* Wills that contain a trust can be more expensive due to their complicated structure. The cost can differ depending upon where the attorney is located: usually, attorneys in larger cities are more expensive because their cost of doing business is greater. As with any fee for services rendered (whether it be a doctor, attorney, or a plumber), consumers should learn as much as they can and even do some comparison shopping before committing themselves.

But let us now take a look at the requirements for a will, what comprises an estate, and what role an executor performs.

2

An Overview of Your Will

PREPARING THE WILL

There is a uniform probate law in the United States upon which most states model their legislation concerning wills. Laws differ from state to state; consequently, there may be some requirements peculiar to your state, and your attorney can explain them. Here are some general legal requirements for a will:

Know what you own and to whom you are leaving your property. This is *testamentary capacity,* which is the minimum amount of intelligence a person must possess to have an enforceable will.

Sign and *date* your will at the end.

Sign your will *voluntarily* thereby asserting that no fraud, duress, or undue influence has been exerted. To be more precise, you have not been tricked or deceived when developing it; no one has threatened you with harm if one or more provisions are not included; and you have not been excessively flattered or pressured into incorporating specific provisions to the benefit or detriment of some third party.

Sign your will in the *presence of witnesses.* Most states require two witnesses; a few states require three. Have the witnesses print their names (in addition to their signatures) and include their addresses. The reason for including the printed name and address is to identify each witness clearly. This is crucial information if witnesses have to be produced in court to testify. More will be said in chapter 3 about witnessing a will.

State to the witnesses that the document is your will and ask them to witness it. This is called *publication.*

The witnesses must be *disinterested,* which generally means that they are not left anything through your will. They must be *adults,* have a reasonable ability to *comprehend* what is happening, and be able to *relate* what is happening.

The *witnesses also must witness each other signing* as witnesses.

Sample Situation

Although a person may dispose of his or her estate in any manner, *there are limits.* Here is a Connecticut case that resulted in a limitation on how an estate could be distributed.

A woman left her estate to a man named John Gale Forbes. She believed he had appeared to her from space when she played with her Ouija board. The evidence showed that she believed Mr. Forbes existed, despite the fact that she knew nothing about him. Her papers made numerous references to him and described the help he had given her during their twenty years of communication. Her executor unsuccessfully tried to establish the existence of John Gale Forbes.

The court decided that the mystical Mr. Forbes was the product of a mental delusion and concluded that the woman lacked testamentary capacity. The will, therefore, was of no consequence (declared null and void). The woman's next of kin received her estate.

Money-Saving Suggestion

Do not try a *do-it-yourself will.* Is a will form purchased at a stationery store sufficient guidance to prepare a will? In some situations it is sufficient; but when it does not work, a major catastrophe can result. *The serious issue of who gets the monetary results of your life requires a visit to an attorney.*

Your visit will save you and your estate more money than the amount of the attorney's fee. There is too much at stake to rely on a standard form. Think of the money the attorney is going to charge your survivors if there is a legal question raised as to whether the will was properly executed and witnessed, and whether those inheriting your assets were clearly identified, or whether a particular asset specifically left to someone was clearly identified. *The cost of preventive law is less than the cost of corrective law.*

A doctor's hope should be that illness is eliminated, and the plumber's hope should be that the pipes do not leak. Similarly, an attorney's hope should be that you do not need an attorney. But when you do need a doctor or a plumber or an attorney, go hire one! *This suggestion will in the long run save you both money and headaches, not to mention relieving survivors of unnecessary frustration.*

YOUR ESTATE

You are reading this book either because you are concerned about what happens to *your* possessions after you are no longer here or because you are concerned about what happens to *someone else's* possessions after he or she is no longer here. No one can be sure that there is life after death. But you can be sure that, wherever you go, *you cannot take your property with you.* You can, however, *determine where your estate goes.*

Thus far, we have learned who receives your estate after you die: *either your next of kin, as defined by state law,* or *those named in your will.* We have also learned the requirements for a will. Now let us consider what comprises an estate.

Here is a list of assets commonly owned: real estate, stocks, bonds, cash, bank accounts, certificates of deposit (CDs), life insurance, retirement benefits, jewelry, furniture, clothes, automobiles, art works, and perhaps a business. Your estate may also include other assets, such as: an income tax refund that you have not yet received, a lease (to an apartment, an automobile, etc.), or a debt someone *owes you. Your estate includes everything you own.* Also, *whatever debts you owe* are part of your estate.

Be sure to discuss with your attorney every possible asset you might own. *Review your ownership documents (titles, bills of sale, mortgages, etc.) with the attorney* (and married couples should review these documents with each other). Keep the originals in a safe deposit box, but be sure that a reliable person close to you knows its location. Make photocopies of these documents and keep them at home. When photocopying the will, *do not* remove the staples. (By removing staples, you open the door to a claim by a disinherited distributee that a page of the original will was removed and a new one was inserted.)

This discussion of estates is a good time to introduce the often confusing subject of *joint ownership* of assets. Consider this frequently asked question: "If my will leaves everything to my sister, *but I have our mother's name on my bank account as a joint owner with the right of survivorship,* then at the time of my death who will receive the bank account?" Your mother will receive the bank account. The ownership of the account, in addition to being a present joint ownership by you and your mother, is also a *future ownership* of the entire account by the eventual survivor of the two joint owners. Therefore, at your death, this *joint account is not distributed by your will,* because you gave the future sole ownership to the other person on the account, namely, your mother. This idea of joint ownership will be reviewed on various occasions throughout this book. But let's take another quick look at this situation.

Sample Situation

The only asset comprising John's estate is a money market account of about $50,000. His will divides his estate evenly between his sisters, Teresa and Mary. However, because John is getting quite frail and has difficulty getting to the bank, he puts Teresa's name on the account as a joint owner. Upon John's death, the money market account probably goes to Teresa, *unless Mary can convince a court that John did this for convenience only.*

Money-Saving Suggestions

After reviewing your estate with an attorney, *you should review your insurance coverage on these items:* Review your *homeowner's insurance* policy. Has it kept up with inflation? Do you need a *valuable items* rider to your policy? This covers items, such as jewelry, which are excluded from homeowner's insurance coverage. Also, review your *automobile insurance.*

Check with your employer to see if you have insurance to cover disability. If you are self-employed, you will most probably want to purchase this insurance. Do you have adequate *health insurance,* including major medical insurance coverage? Do you understand *exactly what this health insurance covers?* Also, reevaluate the amount of *life insurance* to determine if you have ample coverage. Not only will you be missed by those who loved you, but your income will be missed if your loved ones relied on you for financial support. Incidentally, review not only your own life insurance, but also that of the person *you rely upon* for support. Speak to your insurance agent before you have your will prepared. This is the time to obtain answers to all your insurance questions.

Some individuals have too much insurance. Each time they receive information on coverage, especially information about health insurance, they immediately decide to buy it. Exercise your freedom of choice; learn about the coverage before deciding to purchase it. If necessary, have someone review your options with you. Remember, *you have the final word.*

THE PERSONAL REPRESENTATIVE OF THE ESTATE (EXECUTOR OR ADMINISTRATOR)

You have learned of your right to select the person (or bank) who will supervise your estate. *The executor is the person (or bank) named in your will who, after your death, gathers and distributes your assets as directed by your will.* If you die without a will, the court appoints the personal representative of your estate. This is usually your closest relative, and this person is called, not an executor, but an *administrator.*

Although an executor is named in your will, this person (or bank) does not automatically become executor upon your death. The probate court must first determine that your will is a legally valid document. After this occurs, the executor is then authorized to supervise your estate. The court gives the executor a document that in most states is called *letters testamentary* (although referred to in the plural, it is only one piece of paper). The letters testamentary allows the executor to gather the deceased's assets. If you die *without* a will, the person appointed as the administrator of your estate is given *letters of administration.*

Through your executor your wishes are carried out. Whom should you select as executor? This person might be the individual designated to receive the *largest portion* of your estate. If this person is not capable of handling the responsibility, then select some other trusted person as the executor. You could select *someone else who is receiving a legacy,* or your *spouse,* or your *attorney,* or your *bank.* When should there be more than one executor? There is nothing wrong with having two or more executors, who are called *co-executors,* but are they necessary? Co-executors might be necessary if the estate is large (over a few hundred thousand dollars) or unduly complicated (perhaps a business owned by the deceased must be protected by the estate).

Your executor must be honest, efficient, and competent. This person will be your employee after you are dead and will receive a payment called an *executor's commission*. But even though this individual will be paid, as a courtesy you should ask the person if he or she is willing to take the job. Some states (Florida for instance) require an executor to be a state resident. However, there is an exception that allows a close relative, although living in some other state, to serve as executor. The decision on naming your executor is an important one, so give it some serious thought. Remember, a person might be so involved with his or her own life that there is just no time or energy left to be an executor. Part Two discusses the executor's duties (what is called the administration of the estate).

Sample Situation

Joseph's mother has been dead for a while but her estate has dragged on for years. The estate is beset with confusion; friends and relatives are dismayed and angry. Perhaps the estate has an executor who is lazy, incompetent, or devious. Cases like this do occur. *Choose your executor carefully*. Remember, the recalcitrant executor will make life frustrating for those you love—the people named in your will to receive your estate.

Money-Saving Suggestion

Have a successor executor named in your will. If your first choice predeceases (dies before) you or later decides not to take on the responsibility, this suggestion can save you the expense of a *new will*. (A new will must be drawn if *any* change is made in the existing will. Alternatively, a codicil, an amendment to a will, can be drawn, but it, too, requires all of the same formalities as a will.) Here is how my suggestion of a successor executor can be expressed in a will:

> I appoint my uncle JOHN SMITH (give his current address) as my executor. If he predeceases me or is otherwise unable to act as my executor, I appoint my cousin JAMES SMITH (give his current address) as successor executor.

Be mindful that a co-executor is not the same as a successor executor: the former serve together, while a successor executor takes the place of an executor who had died or is otherwise unable to act as executor. Here is an example of *co-executors* and a *successor executor* expressed in a will:

I appoint my uncles JOHN SMITH (give his current address) and WILLIAM SMITH (give his current address) as my co-executors. If either one predeceases me or is otherwise unable to act as my executor, I appoint my cousin JAMES SMITH (give his current address) as successor executor.

Before considering whether you should appoint a bank as your executor, here is a suggestion about something that, although quite obvious, is sometimes overlooked. If you decide to have co-executors, *choose people who can work together.* Most people know a great deal about their potential executors, through long associations, family ties, or strong friendships. Therefore, when considering co-executors, it should be easy to determine if the candidates will be compatible. Co-executors who fail to cooperate often find themselves embroiled in lengthy and costly court battles.

A BANK AS EXECUTOR

I like the idea of a bank as executor, especially when there are substantial assets. But even when large estates are not involved, there are still sound reasons for using a bank. Here are some reasons given by my clients over the years: (1) to preserve a business after death; (2) no close relative or friend is willing to serve in the capacity of executor; (3) potential conflict might arise between those designated to receive assets; (4) a testamentary trust is involved [see the end of Part One]; (5) preservation of the estate's assets requires constant supervision; (6) grandparents are leaving their estate to grandchildren; (7) assets are being left to a resident of a foreign country; and (8) a bank's estate and trust department has the necessary experience to accomplish the job in an *efficient* and *competent manner.*

The executor represents all who may claim an interest in the deceased's estate, including the *creditors* of the deceased and also those named as the *recipients of your property.* The executor represents the total mass of interests and not one against the other. Therefore, a bank might be better suited to this job than a relative, who may find it difficult dealing with the various people interested in your estate.

The bank, like any other executor, *receives a fee* for serving in this capacity—as well it should. Often it is the same fee an individual executor receives; in some cases the fee is slightly higher. The executor's fee is usually a percentage of the estate, and is in the range of four percent for estates valued at under one million dollars. As with anything else, be a smart consumer. First, determine whether your spouse, adult child, or close friend has the time, talent, integrity, and willingness to serve as executor. If so, then name this person as executor. But you might find yourself in need of a bank as executor. If so, shop around until *you find a bank with which you are comfortable.*

Here are five reasons for choosing a bank as your executor: (1) a bank performs this function as a *full-time job;* (2) a bank's performance is *audited* by two and sometimes three groups (in addition to the beneficiary's surveillance): internal bank auditors, state bank regulators, and sometimes federal regulators; (3) a bank has a *continuity of existence,* unlike your individual executor who may predecease you; (4) a bank *continues doing business within the state,* whereas your individual executor might move out of state, thus becoming disqualified as an executor or making it inconvenient for the estate; (5) a bank has better *staffing* than an individual executor.

Most banks do not want to be named as executor unless there are potential estate assets of at least a few hundred thousand dollars. Ask about this minimum amount when you inquire into the bank's fee for serving as executor.

Sample Situation

I share with you the following letter, which I recently wrote to some clients:

Dear Mr. and Mrs. Client:
    As you requested, here is a summary of what we discussed this past week about naming your bank as successor executor in each of your wills:

1. The bank will be the executor only after both of you are gone. Then the bank will gather the assets, prepare and file all required tax returns, do all the investment and administrative work—which, unfortunately, is quite involved in estate administration—and distribute the assets quickly and efficiently to your children and other legatees.

2. The bank, during the period it serves as executor, will be in frequent consultation with your children and other legatees.

3. The bank's fee is tax deductible.

4. Reasons for having a bank, rather than one of your out-of-state heirs, as the executor:

a. The bank functions as executor efficiently, quickly, and correctly. It does this full-time and is good at what it does. Otherwise, one or more of your children will be doing this administrative work. Incidentally, the bank is held to a higher degree of responsibility and accountability as compared to an individual executor.

b. Your money, therefore, gets to your children more quickly than if they try to do the administrative work themselves.

c. Most clients with substantial wealth use the services of a bank because it is a convenience.

d. The bank has professional expertise in the stock and bond markets, which is critical given the make-up of your estate assets. An individual executor would be faced with the potential hiring of an investment advisor. On this subject of retaining professional help, an individual executor most likely would also have to retain the services of an accountant and a temporary custodian of the assets. All of this at a cost to the estate. With the bank, *all* administrative services are inclusive.

5. Finally, given the time constraints inherent in the professional lives of your children and their spouses, can we really be sure that they will have the time that is so critical to an effective estate settlement?

As your lawyer, I recommend that the bank be named as successor executor in the will of each of you. To repeat what I wrote at the outset, this means that the bank will serve as executor only in the estate of the survivor of you. As the bank explained to you and your children when it stated its fee, this fee will be paid only when and if it serves as executor. But from my experience, a bank earns this fee, and this is an opinion also shared by many families.

Money-Saving Suggestion

After what I have just written, the following suggestion might seem surprising. Do not name a bank to serve as your executor if you have a competent and honest spouse, relative, or friend who is *willing* and *able* to assume this responsibility. The bank could be named to serve as successor executor, if the person you name as executor predeceases you.

A situation might arise where, for example, a spouse and a bank are serving as co-executors, and the spouse *wants to replace the bank* with another co-executor of his or her choosing. This can be accomplished if the will provides for it and if the bank does not object to the inclusion of this clause:

> My co-executor spouse is authorized, with absolute discretion, to appoint a successor bank co-executor to act in place of the bank co-executor then acting. This can be done by delivering to the bank co-executor, then acting, a letter naming the successor bank as co-executor and by delivering a duplicate of this letter to the successor bank co-executor.

If you are thinking about appointing a bank as your executor, educate yourself about the estate departments of banks. Interview a few of them; *do not be shy with your questions;* carefully evaluate and compare the answers you are given.

Though finding a willing and qualified executor may not be easy, once the selection has been made, many people feel that a considerable weight has been lifted from their shoulders. But what few realize is that this decision, though a major one, is merely one step in the process of preparing a will, a process that has only just begun. Now that you know who will carry out your wishes after your death, it is time to consider to whom those assets will be distributed.

PEOPLE WHO INHERIT (LEGATEES)

A *legatee* is a person who inherits money or other property through a will. In your will, be sure to identify specifically all your legatees. For example, if a legatee is a relative, *identify the relationship.* Remember, people often leave legacies to relatives, and sometimes there is more than one relative with the same name. Another way to be clear about the identity of your chosen legatees, whether or not they are relatives, is to *include their current addresses.* If a question later arises as to which John Jones your will refers to, the John Jones who lives at that address, or at one time lived at that address, will prevail.

Should you have many legatees in your will? *It is up to you: it is your money and you can do with it what you want.* You can leave it to one person or to a number of people. (One person, however, who is protected from being disinherited is your spouse, and we shall look at this situation shortly.) Many people equate fairness with equality, and conclude that if they have three children, one-third of the estate should be left to each child. If you wish to leave your estate equally among the three children, that is fine. But do not feel pressured or constrained to abide by some artificial formula. Some people reward successful friends or relatives with a legacy; others reward the ne'er-do-well with a legacy. I judge neither extreme, but I admire the confidence these people have in their own decisions. They are not pressured by unwritten, and sometimes inappropriate, rules of conduct; *they make up their own minds.*

Some attorneys assume an expansive role in will preparation: their advice goes far beyond the *how to* of will preparation to include the subject of *to whom* clients should leave their possessions. While there is nothing wrong with this expanded role, in my opinion the attorney's role in the selection of legatees should be limited. Decisions relating to the transfer of wealth are personal. Sometimes being a *good listener* is the best way to help a person who is trying to make a decision. The attorney (or anyone who might be offering advice to a person who is planning on having a will prepared) should *reinforce* the person's confidence and *encourage* the individual to make a decision based on a combination of thoughtful deliberation and emotion.

Sample Situation

Look at your will to see if the current addresses of your legatees are correctly stated. If any addresses are incorrect, do not change anything in the will. Write and advise your *executor* of the correct addresses. Furthermore, if any of the addresses of the legatees are incorrectly stated, *ask your attorney* if this might cause a problem in the future identification of these individuals. There are many cases of inadequately or incorrectly identified legatees. The case of the missing or incorrect address presents these two possible problems: First, will the executor be able to *locate* the person(s)? Second, will there be a question as to whether the person eventually located is the *same person who is named in your will?*

Money-Saving Suggestions

I have suggested that you name a successor executor in your will. I also suggest that you name *successor legatees,* because you might outlive those whom you initially expected to inherit your estate. Here is an example of how successor legatees are named in a will:

To my nephew JOHN SMITH (give his current address) I bequeath my Steinway piano. If he predeceases me, I bequeath my Steinway piano to my niece MARY SMITH (give her current address).

At the time the will is being drafted, some people are only conscious of their own death; they hesitate to name successor legatees. These people believe that they are going to die soon, or at least *sooner than those named as legatees in the will.* But most people live many years after executing a will, and *the probability of outliving one or more of the legatees is quite high.* This is clearly apparent if you imagine a family gathering in honor of the ninety-year-old patriarch, and many of the people at the gathering are the patriarch's legatees. Although the patriarch has the *shortest* life expectancy, surely it is not certain that he will be the *next* family member to die. I recommend that for each legatee named in your will, you consider naming a successor legatee.

This suggestion saves you the cost of revising your will each time a legatee predeceases you. But what happens if you leave your diamond necklace to Mary, and you do not name a successor legatee to receive the necklace if Mary predeceases you? Then, if Mary *does predecease you,* this diamond necklace will be part of your residuary estate, which is the next topic we will discuss.

Before moving on, here is another thought. This suggestion—naming successor legatees in the event that *you outlive some or all of those whom you designated as primary legatees*—should remind you of the obvious reality of the situation. It explodes the myth that preparing a will somehow *hastens your death.*

THE MOST IMPORTANT CLAUSE (RESIDUARY CLAUSE)

Wills have a residuary (or remainder) clause, *which distributes estate assets not otherwise left to someone.* It may be the most important clause in the whole document, because it could distribute the bulk of a person's assets. Perhaps you are familiar with the expression, "All the rest, residue, and remainder of my estate I give, devise, and bequeath to. . . ." In the language of a will, this is how the residuary clause begins. Attorneys sometimes use many words where a few would suffice. The same direction could be expressed, "I give the rest of my estate to. . . ." (Incidentally, land and buildings are *devised;* everything else is *bequeathed.*)

Suppose you want your nephew, your niece, and your friend to share in your estate equally; if one of them predeceases you, *you want the remaining two to share your estate equally;* if two of them predecease you, *you want the survivor to receive it all.* Here is how you express this intent in your residuary clause:

> All the rest, residue, and remainder of my estate I give, devise, and bequeath in equal shares to the following individuals *who survive me:* my nephew (give name and address), my niece (give name and address), and my friend (give name and address).

If you *fail to have a residuary clause* in your will, then all of your estate assets are not distributed through your will. Suppose, for example, that you leave $25,000 to your sister Mary, that you have no residuary clause, and at your death you are worth $100,000. Who receives the $75,000? It is received by your next of kin. Perhaps the good sister Mary and brother Charlie share the $75,000.

Remember to have a residuary clause. In general, you name your most loved person or persons in the residuary clause. Your wealth may substantially increase between the time you write your will and the time of your death. It is this residuary clause that distributes these estate assets. The importance of naming your most loved person(s) in the residuary clause is shown in the following sample situation. Sometimes naming someone who is not close to you as residuary legatee *is even worse than having no residuary clause.*

Sample Situation

Margaret has a net worth of about $100,000, and in her will she leaves this sum to good sister Mary. She has a brother, evil Charlie, and she wants to leave him the *current miniscule balance* of her assets—maybe a few hundred dollars. Margaret, mistakenly, *names her brother as the residuary legatee.* Ten years later Margaret dies; her estate is worth $300,000. Her sister receives $100,000; her evil brother receives $200,000!!

This was not Margaret's intent. Her mistake was in not naming the most loved person(s) in the residuary clause. Remember that the residuary clause distributes the *additional estate assets you obtained after you signed your will.* Therefore, do not use this residuary clause to distribute the small current balance of your estate assets not otherwise distributed through your will. You may win a lottery, and what remains of this additional wealth at the time of your death goes to your residuary legatee(s).

Money-Saving Suggestion

Suppose you leave your residuary estate to your nephew, your niece, and your friend. If your nephew predeceases you, do you want your niece and your friend to share your entire residuary estate, as in the earlier example? Or do you want your nephew's share to go to someone else? If you want it to go to someone else, this can be handled by naming a *successor residuary legatee*. This can be accomplished by using the following clause:

> All the rest, residue, and remainder I leave as follows: *one-third* to my nephew (give name and address), but if he predeceases me, this one-third is to go to my brother (give name and address); *one-third* to my niece (give name and address), but if she predeceases me, this one-third is to go to ABC charity (give address), for its general purposes; *one-third* to my friend (give name and address), but if my friend predeceases me, this one-third is to go to another friend (give name and address).

Remember, you have these two choices: you can name *successor residuary legatees,* as in the above example, or you can decide to have the *surviving residuary legatees* share your residuary estate, as in the earlier example. Decide now what you want, and express this decision in your will. This decision might save you the expense of a new will (or codicil) if a residuary legatee predeceases you.

Our discussion of legatees and your residuary estate is now complete. But what of all those potential legatees who didn't find their way into your will?

DISINHERITED RELATIVES

In many states a spouse cannot be disinherited, and must receive a mandated minimum share of the deceased spouse's estate. Many states call this minimum share the *spouse's elective share,* which could be, for example, one-third of the deceased spouse's estate, or one-half of the deceased spouse's estate, or whatever the state law stipulates. The spouse can elect to take this mandated minimum share and thus not be limited to the amount left as a legacy. *Find out what protection surviving spouses are offered by your state.* Be aware that the surviving spouse's elective share is reduced if the deceased spouse is survived by children.

Notice that *elective share* and *intestate share* refer to entirely different situations. *Elective share* is what a surviving spouse receives if the deceased husband/wife dies *with a will* that leaves less to the survivor than is guaranteed by state law. The surviving spouse then *elects* to take the higher alternative amount guaranteed by state law. An *intestate share* is what the surviving husband/wife receives when the deceased spouse dies *without a will*. Often, however, the elective share and the intestate share are the *same percentage* of the deceased spouse's estate, although they refer to two entirely different situations.

Perhaps you have heard of a *postnuptial (or prenuptial) agreement*. In this agreement between husband and wife (or entered into by those who are soon to become husband and wife), each can agree to give up this elective share protection. The result of this voluntary waiver of the protection of state law is that *a spouse can then be disinherited.*

Now what about disinheriting the rest of the world other than your spouse? In just about all state jurisdictions, there is no problem in disinheriting a child, a parent, or any other relative. Should you specifically mention a disliked relative and then leave that relative nothing, or perhaps the sum of one dollar? I advise that you do so only if your state requires that your child must be specifically excluded or, if not so excluded, will otherwise share in your estate. *In any other situation it is not necessary to leave someone a dollar.* It does, however, answer a potential challenge that some page of the will has been lost and that is why the challenger is not mentioned. This lost page argument is so weak that it does not need a response. But by leaving a person the sum of one dollar, however, you answer the challenge. There is no need to state the reason for bequeathing only one dollar (or nothing) to one or more people, but some persons like to give a lengthy explanation. Be careful, however, that you do not libel the person receiving the one dollar. (We will look at libel in chapter 8.) In summary, in most situations, the legacy of one dollar is merely an attempt to write *a few piercing final comments.*

Sample Situation

Have you heard the story of the man who asked a relative to remember him in the will? The will had the following provision: "To my relative who asked to be remembered in my will, *I remember you;* this is the reason why I leave you nothing." Nasty, but subtle last words.

The more serious situation is *your rights* upon death of your spouse (or upon divorce). The law in each state is different, particularly in states known as community-property states. So check with your attorney to find out what protection is provided by your state.

Money-Saving Suggestion

A *nuptial agreement* should include the following statements: each spouse is familiar with the other spouse's assets (which should be listed); each spouse is aware of what *protection* state law gives to a spouse; each spouse enters into the agreement *voluntarily; each spouse waives a minimum share of the other's estate* (although each spouse may voluntarily leave the other spouse a legacy). Each party to such an agreement should have a different attorney review the document before it is signed. This avoids the future claim that an attorney, if shared by the couple, did not fairly represent both parties. Often this claim has merit, particularly if the attorney, shared by the couple, has had a long and close relationship with one spouse and is paid by that spouse.

For a late-in-life marriage, especially where there are children from previous marriages, a nuptial agreement can prove useful. It helps to prevent future family fights, including a potential court battle over a will. *Adult children from the earlier marriages are much more receptive to a parent's impending marriage when there is a nuptial agreement.* It is also a practical arrangement; partners in a late-in-life marriage often decide to keep their first fortunes totally separate from the finances of the new marriage.

Some elderly clients have asked for my thoughts regarding their children's or grandchildren's nuptial agreement. When asked, I offer two opinions:

First, I am not too enthusiastic about a nuptial agreement between younger people. In some situations, no agreement is needed; the pending marriage should be delayed or cancelled. This becomes apparent when the young, poor couple begins to fight over who is to retain possession of items (some of which are not yet owned) *when* they get divorced. The anticipated short duration of the commitment is revealed by the frequency of the use of the word "when."

Second, I often suggest that these older clients stop worrying about their children and grandchildren and concentrate on their own well-being. It is time for elderly adults to look after their own affairs; their good job of raising and seeing to the needs of their children is over. In turn, these children will do the same good job in nurturing the grandchildren. Sometimes the elderly client is so happy with my first opinion (because the client shares it) that my second opinion is embraced wholeheartedly.

From executor and legatees we now move on to those who will attest to the existence of this, your will. These are the *witnesses*.

3

Witnesses to Your Will

THE FUNCTION OF A WITNESS

A will must be witnessed. *In most states two witnesses are required;* in a few states three witnesses are needed. The witnesses must be adults with a *minimum standard of intelligence;* they must be aware that a *will is being signed,* and they must be able to *relate what happened.* The witnesses are witnessing that

(1) the person is *signing* the will;

(2) the person signing the will is signing it *voluntarily;* that is, no fraud, duress, or undue influence is being exerted on the person signing the will;

(3) the person signing the will appears to know the nature and the consequences of the document (as you know, this is called *testamentary capacity*);

(4) the person signing the will says to the witnesses that the document being signed is a will and asks the witnesses to witness the signature (as you know, this is called *publication*);

(5) the *other witnesses* are signing as witnesses.

The signatures of the testator and the witnesses are not notarized. However, there is another document that some states require at the testator's death. It is a notarized statement, signed by the witnesses, that summarizes what was observed. This notarized statement is called the *affidavit of the witnesses.* In some states the testator also signs this document. A will with this affidavit is called a *self-proved will.*

Although this affidavit of the witnesses does not have to be produced until the time of the testator's death, some states, including Connecticut, Florida, New Jersey, and New York, allow it to be obtained at the time the will is signed. This is very convenient, because if the affidavit of the witnesses is obtained when the will is signed, then after the testator's death the witnesses do not have to be located.

Death, hopefully, will be in the distant future. Therefore, it is desirable to obtain this affidavit of the witnesses at the same time the will is signed, rather than waiting until the testator's death. Even if the executor then finds the witnesses, there is the possibility they *might not remember what happened:* Did they witness the testator signing the will? Did they witness each other signing the will as witnesses? Did the testator have testamentary capacity, and did he or she sign the will voluntarily (without fraud, duress, or undue influence)? Was the will published: did the testator advise the witnesses that the document is the testator's will, and did the testator request the witnesses to witness the signing?

Here are some additional thoughts on your witnesses:

(1) A person who is left a legacy by you cannot be a witness to your will.

(2) Your executor can be a witness to your will.

(3) It is advisable (because it is an important legal document) for you to have not only the minimum two or three witnesses that your state requires, but also one additional witness.

(4) Your witnesses *do not have to know your financial situation or the contents of your will.*

I stated that a person who is left a legacy cannot be a witness to your will. There might be an exception to this rule in your state, and the explanation that follows will also help you become familiar with the legal terminology learned thus far.

Let us assume that Peter witnesses his widowed father's will, that he is his father's only distributee, and that the will leaves everything to him—except $10,000, which has been left to charity. In this situation, Peter, a legatee, can be a witness to the will. Why? If the amount a legatee receives through a will is *less than the potential intestate share* (the share the legatee is likely to receive if no will existed), then the legatee can be a witness. Peter does not benefit from the will's existence; in fact, he is financially deprived by it. (He would have gotten more from his father's estate had no will existed.) Despite this possible exception, I advise that you *have neither legatee(s) nor distributee(s) as witnesses to your will.*

Sample Situations

Mary has died, but the witnesses to her will have also died. They had not signed an affidavit of the witnesses when they witnessed Mary's will many years ago. Is Mary's will still legally effective? Yes. The validity of the signature of each witness can be verified, one hopes (perhaps by comparing the signature of the witness with another signature that a bank might have on file). But if that will is challenged by the next of kin, the attorney for the estate will be wishing he had *a witness to the event or an affidavit of the witnesses.*

There is a short sample will in the appendix to this book. At the end of it is an affidavit of the witnesses (see p. 217). Take a look at these legal documents. Some words of caution, however: *do not use them as a sample for a homemade will or an affidavit of witnesses.* I include them only to make this book more understandable. Remember that not only do laws differ from state to state, but individual needs differ as well. Wills should be custom-made to fit the special circumstances of the testator.

Money-Saving Suggestion

Make sure you have the affidavit of the witnesses to your will. Not only does this save your executor the time and the expense of locating the witnesses years later, it also avoids the problems of the dead witness and the forgetful witness, neither of whom can give credibility to the will.

If you do not have the affidavit of the witnesses, write to your attorney today and ask why you do not have it. If you are a resident of a state that requires this affidavit and allows it to be signed before your death, *then have this document signed now. Years from now it will save your estate time and money.* It is also a convenience to the witnesses. They can witness a will and not have to travel to court, perhaps from a distant location, at some time in the future.

Let us now discuss having your *attorney as a witness.*

THE ATTORNEY AS A WITNESS

The attorney is not a witness unless he or she specifically signs the will as a witness. Let us assume that the attorney is standing in the office with the testator and two secretaries; the testator is signing the will, and the two secretaries are signing as witnesses. In this example, the attorney is not considered to be a witness, because the attorney does not sign the will as a witness to the document. *Nothing prohibits an attorney from being a witness to a will that he or she has prepared;* however, the attorney must sign the will as a witness.

It is customary for the attorney to provide the witnesses to your will; usually it is the attorney and members of his or her staff. There is no need for you to impose upon your neighbors by asking them to be witnesses; furthermore, it is none of their business that you are executing a will.

Sample Situations

I mentioned that an attorney should know a great deal about clients who ask to have a will prepared. Be candid with your attorney regarding your net worth. *Do not exaggerate or underestimate your assets.* The attorney should know not only your *general financial situation,* but also any particular problems or unusual circumstances surrounding your finances, so that these situations can be properly resolved. I mention this because some people still think that attorneys will charge wealthier clients more than those persons who are less well off. At the time your will is prepared, tell the attorney your actual net worth and ask about the lawyer's fee for drawing up the document. If you do not like the fee, go to someone else. Full disclosure is in your best interest: terrible mistakes can be made in situations where people underestimate their net worth. *Tax planning is then made on the basis of erroneous information.* An even worse situation is where there is no tax planning, because the attorney is not aware that the net worth exceeds the amount that can be left free of tax at death. The risks of being less than candid may be far greater than you ever expected. *Do not hide anything.*

Also be candid with your attorney on any particular family problem. What you tell the attorney is kept in confidence. Do not hestitate to tell the attorney (if applicable) that you have a few extra spouses or a few extra children. Perhaps there are relatives who are indebted to you, or you to them. It is appropriate and necessary for the attorney to learn about these situations now, because they can affect your eventual estate and the estate plan now being formulated.

Money-Saving Suggestion

There are legal methods to reduce the various taxes that confront estates and legatees. For this reason, the topic of taxation will be brought up occasionally, as the need arises, throughout Parts One and Two of this book. Then in Part Three the subject of taxation will be explored in further detail. At this point, however, I want to familiarize you with the various *categories of taxes* that might be encountered:

1. the deceased's *federal individual income tax* for the year of death (and perhaps the previous year if, for example, the death occurred before April 15th);

2. the *state individual income tax* if the deceased was domiciled in a state that taxes income (some states, like Florida, do not have an income tax);

3. the *federal estate tax,* which happens when the taxable estate of the deceased *exceeds $600,000;* but *everything left to a surviving spouse is exempt from estate tax;* [To any married reader who is a noncitizen of the United States or whose spouse is a noncitizen: Our tax law discriminates against noncitizen spouses who receive property from their spouse (whether through a gift or at time of death). So keep in mind that whenever I make a reference to married people, I am assuming that the receiving spouse is a United States citizen. Let me also point out that this discrimination can be alleviated by establishing a Qualified Domestic Trust (QDT). Although I will not be discussing it here, you might want to ask your attorney about a QDT.]

4. a *state estate tax* based on the value of the estate's assets; [This tax is triggered in some states at a much lower valuation than the federal estate tax.]

5. an *inheritance tax* on *those who receive a deceased's assets;* [However, these states generally exempt, in whole or in part, property received by spouses, children, and grandchildren.]

6. if the estate generates income during its administration, a *federal estate income tax;*

7. if the state has an income tax, a *state estate income tax;*

8. the *gift tax*, which is a tax paid by the person *making the gift* (for gifts in excess of $10,000); [The reason for this tax is to prevent an avoidance of estate tax.]

9. an income tax that the legatee(s) or distributee(s) might have to pay on income earned by the estate during administration and distributed to them.

With this general idea of taxes, let us return to wills and take a look at some of the problems to avoid.

4

Problems to Avoid

SOME DRAFTING PITFALLS

A will communicates the testator's intentions. Here are some pitfalls to avoid.

If you leave something to *someone's spouse,* be specific as to the person in question: Do you mean the current spouse or perhaps a later one? This confusion occurs in the following bequest: "I leave $10,000 to my friend Harry Friendly's wife." If you want to leave something to Harry Friendly's wife, let us call her Bertha, then refer to her as Bertha and not chauvinistically as Harry Friendly's wife. Alternatively, if you want to leave something to the person married to Harry Friendly at the time of your death (whether Bertha or someone else), then refer to this person as "the person married to Harry Friendly at the time of my death."

If something is left to a *named employee,* must this person be in the testator's employ at death? For example, it would be very confusing if your will read: "I leave $10,000 to Harry Friendly, who has been and always will be my loyal employee." If he *does* have to be your employee at the time of your death to inherit the $10,000, then say so, like this: "I leave $10,000 to Harry Friendly, but only on the condition that he is employed by me at the time of my death." If he *does not* have to be your employee at your death to inherit, make this clear by not mentioning that "he has been and always will be my loyal employee."

Never leave "my cash on hand" to someone, because few people will know what you mean. Does this include bank accounts? Does it include cash in the cash register of your store? Does it include cash in a safe deposit box? Who knows? "Contents of my home" is also unnecessarily vague. Does this phrase include a painting on the wall? Probably. Does it include your General Motors stock certificates located in the bureau drawer? Probably not. It is confusing.

Do not leave your 1991 Chevrolet to someone; refer to it as the "automobile owned at my death." Otherwise, if you die several years from now, unless you still own the 1991 Chevrolet, your named legatee will not receive it. Even worse, your named legatee will not receive the 2021 Chevrolet you might own at your death.

Sample Situation

Wirsig's estate, a case litigated in Nebraska, is about a will with a serious omission. Twenty dollars was bequeathed to an individual. But the will also contained this direction: "I hereby bequeath and devise all my personal property and all my real property with the exception of twenty dollars." This is an *incomplete sentence;* the will does not identify who receives everything else *other than* the twenty dollars. Who receives the balance, or residue, of the estate?

The court decided that where a testator fails to identify a beneficiary in the will, the court cannot review any additional evidence to determine the identity of a beneficiary. The court reached this decision despite evidence from sources outside the will that the testator's intent was to leave all his property, except the twenty dollars, to his wife. An unfortunate result: make sure your will does not have a similar drafting error.

Money-Saving Suggestion

If you do not understand your will, do not expect other people to understand it. If other people do not understand your will, then after your death a court will attempt to construe what you meant. This court proceeding is called a *construction proceeding,* in which the court looks only at the will to decide what you meant when you created the will. Thus, you cannot rely on the court to correct omissions in your will; moreover, this court proceeding is costly because it can be quite time-consuming.

There are two general areas in which a will might be unclear: (1) the description of the *person* who is to receive something, or (2) the description of the *something* that is to be received. Make sure that *everyone* and *everything* in the will is clearly identified. Only attorneys benefit from a construction proceeding. Do not let it happen to your estate. You have learned the importance of discussing family and personal affairs with your attorney. You have also learned the importance of *making sure you understand each sentence, word, and paragraph of the document.* Do not have these efforts go to waste by signing a will that contains obvious oversights.

MORE DRAFTING PITFALLS

Leaving someone all the AT&T stock you own at the time of your death might someday cause a problem. Does this person receive the corporate stock in an AT&T spin-off company, shares of whose stock you might own at the time of your death? Not necessarily. Although you can leave stock in specific companies to a legatee, future corporate reorganizations (or your sale of the stock) might result in your legatee receiving a dramatically diminished legacy (or none at all). We will take a further look at this situation in chapter 14, in our discussion of "Too Few Assets."

Leaving someone your certificate of deposit at Chase Manhattan Bank is a similar potential pitfall. Suppose you transfer these funds to Chemical Bank. The legatee who is left the Chase Manhattan Bank certificate of deposit does not receive it if you do not own a Chase Manhattan Bank certificate of deposit at your death. It is better to leave a *specific dollar amount,* rather than a particular certificate of deposit.

Leaving *less than or more than one hundred percent of your residuary estate* is carelessness. If your residuary estate is divided into percentages, make sure they add up to one hundred percent. Avoid a mistake such as leaving eighty percent to Mary and thirty percent to William. Two similar mistakes—the *missing paragraph* and the *missing page*—also occur. These are the subjects of the next sample situations.

Leaving something to your friend without further identifying the friend, perhaps by listing the individual's current address, is a drafting pitfall that could have chaotic results. Suppose, for example, that two individuals with the same name claim to have been the friend or relative named in your will? Without an address to verify the correct legatee, it might be difficult to determine the identity of this person.

Leaving money to a *group of people*—the specific members of which are bunched in a confusing sentence—often has problematic results. Here is an example of such a confusing sentence: "I leave $10,000 to the following: *the children of my brother Robert, and my brother John.*" There are two problems here: is $10,000 the total amount to go to the group, or is $10,000 to go to each member of the group? Is money being left to John or to the children of John (the comma after Robert is crucial)? Read the confusing sentence again, and you will recognize these two pitfalls.

Sample Situations

Court cases describe basic oversights that appear in wills. These oversights include a *missing paragraph* or a *missing page* of the document.

The example of a missing paragraph can be found in a will in which each paragraph is numbered, but one paragraph number is missing. Perhaps paragraph THIRD is followed by paragraph FIFTH. The relative not named in the will may claim that paragraph FOURTH is devoted exclusively *to lovable him or her.*

The example of a page being absent in a will may occur when the document has each page numbered, but one number is missing. Perhaps page THREE is followed by page FIVE. If the text flows clearly from page THREE to page FIVE, this is evidence that a page has *not* been removed from the will; the pages are simply misnumbered. Again, however, the lovable one can now claim that a full page is devoted exclusively *to him or her.*

Try explaining to a relative who has been left out of the will that these inaccuracies are only insignificant oversights by the proofreader. The forgotten relative will forever believe that his or her legacy was contained in missing paragraphs or pages. The court will probably not listen to the cry of this disinherited person; it will probably agree with the nominated executor that the will is complete. But why risk the cost of a court proceeding? Careful proofreading is a must.

Money-Saving Suggestion

Do not rush any stage of the will-preparation process. It is an important document. That one final office conference may be crucial to assure a properly prepared will. While word-processing equipment makes it easier to revise drafts of a will, this technological advance has brought with it a drawback. Suppose you are at the attorney's office and are ready to sign your will, but decide suddenly to make a last-minute change. These quick revisions are just the occasions when mistakes can be made. I suggest that if you make a last-minute change, delay signing your will; take the new draft home with you and take a day or two to make sure that the revised will expresses your intentions. When you are sure, return to the attorney's office for the signing and witnessing of the will. But do not let too much time elapse between office visits. Remember that during the interval either *no will exists* or *some prior will is still in force*—a will that may not reflect your current wishes for the distribution of your assets.

Perhaps the reason you decided on a last-minute change was because you had not given enough thought to including some instructions in your will the first time it was drawn—for example, the disposition of your household furniture. The next chapter will consider some of these instructions.

5

Special Instructions

FURNITURE AND PERSONAL EFFECTS

In your will there should be a paragraph, or perhaps a few paragraphs, stating who receives your clothing, furniture, books, paintings, jewelry, silverware, automobile, and other personal items. I find this clause useful:

> I give and bequeath all my tangible personal effects, *including* clothing, furniture, books, paintings, silverware, (and whatever else you want to *include*), but *excluding* cash, securities, any other monetary instruments, jewelry, automobiles, (and whatever else you want to *exclude*) to (name the person), now residing at (person's address), if this person survives me. My estate shall pay the reasonable cost of moving these items. (In another paragraph, name the people who are to receive the jewelry, automobiles, and whatever other items have been excluded from this clause.)

The law of your state may require that some of these items be left to a surviving spouse as part of what is called a *homestead right.* Otherwise, you have flexibility. But spell out who gets what.

What about leaving items such as furniture or jewelry *equally* to two individuals, perhaps your two children? In such a case, consider giving your executor the authority to make the final decision in the event that the two individuals cannot agree on a fair division of the items. Alternatively, consider leaving items such as furniture or jewelry to just one individual to avoid a division problem. Of course, if you want a particular person to receive a valuable item, such as a ring, clearly identify it and who gets it. To avoid confusion, be sure the identification is sufficient *to distinguish the item in question from any similar items.*

I recommend that you try to *limit the number of people* who are to receive your furniture and other personal effects. As the number of recipients increases, your executor is burdened with the responsibility of attempting to place the objects with those for whom they are intended. Naming so many people is an indication that you are *trying too hard* to have a will that is *perfectly fair*—an impossible goal to achieve.

Sample Situations

A judge, so the story goes, could not get two brothers to agree to an equal distribution of furniture. The disagreement revolved around an antique rocking chair. Neither brother was willing to sell his half of the rocker to the other. The judge brought the matter to a conclusion when he threatened to *break the antique rocker in half.* The brothers quickly found a way to settle their disagreement.

A less intimidating way of settling this type of dispute is to agree on the value of a contested item. Then, by the flip of a coin, decide who is to be the seller. This is a variation of the device used by a parent whose two children argue over the relative sizes of cake slices. The parent tells one child to cut the cake and allows the other child to get the first choice.

The expense of shipping furniture to a legatee can also cause a problem. The legatee usually bears the expense of insuring and shipping the furniture. But to avoid any controversy, *the will should state whether the estate or the legatee is to pay the expenses incidental to delivering the furniture to its final destination.*

Money-Saving Suggestion

In preparing your will you should give serious consideration to *not* identifying each item of jewelry, clothing, and furniture. An identification could result in a higher appraisal value of your estate, thereby triggering a higher estate tax. There is a natural tendency to presume a high value for items specifically described in your will. When the executor then submits a low valuation to the taxation authority, it is suspect. I am not advising tax fraud, just common sense. *Costume jewelry should not be identified in the will;* if it is, no one can fault the state or federal tax auditor for being suspicious of a low valuation.

Items of small economic value (although of high emotional value) should perhaps be left to one person. You can then leave a note (which I refer to as a *letter of intent*) to this person, and suggest how you would like these items distributed. Even better, you could make a gift of these items now, *so that both you and the recipient can share this pleasure of giving and receiving.* There is also the additional incentive of reducing the value of your eventual estate, thereby saving the estate some tax. But more on this in Part Three on taxation.

Let us take a look at this *letter of intent.*

LETTER OF INTENT

Have you written a *letter of intent* to your son or daughter, the contents of which are to be read after your death? Perhaps the letter advises your child on how to spend the legacy; perhaps it suggests that some small item received by the legatee be given as a gift to a third party. Whatever its content, this letter is *not legally binding.* Generally, I do not recommend letters of intent to my clients. If what you have to say is important, then put it in the will. I *do recommend its use,* however, in *two situations.*

The first is where there are a few pieces of *jewelry,* none very expensive, but each with sentimental value. Consider leaving all the jewelry to one person and then, through a letter of intent, suggest who are to receive the various pieces. The benefit of this approach is the *ease with which the executor can distribute the jewelry* to the one person named in the will.

The other situation is that of a *legacy to children.* Suppose Grandma has collectibles, e.g., silver coins, and she wants each grandchild to receive an equal share of the coins. If Grandma leaves the coins "to her grandchildren," two problems could arise. The first and more serious problem occurs if any of the grandchildren are minors. In probating the will, the court may appoint a guardian, perhaps *a different guardian for each minor grandchild,* to assure that the child receives the legacy. This results in unnecessary expenses for the estate and intrusion of a stranger into the family's finances. We already know the second difficulty, which I call the rocking chair problem: *dividing these coins evenly among the grandchildren.* Perhaps Grandma should leave the silver coins to her most trustworthy child, with a letter of intent stating that she hopes these coins will be distributed equally among her grandchildren. This advice is given to save unnecessary legal fees.

The following suggestion is offered in the hope of saving survivors some anguish. Do not leave a letter of intent that recites why you love or hate someone, or a letter that explains some pleasant or painful experience. It is unfair to your survivors, because they cannot respond. There is a poignant scene in Neil Simon's play *Broadway Bound* about such a letter from a father to his son. The father wanted to explain everything; the son reads the letter and disdainfully announces that the letter explains nothing.

Sample Situation

A client enters an attorney's office with a look of anticipation. A happy look! After all, he has his grandmother's letter, which clearly states, "I love you; I leave you everything; this letter is to be considered my will." The letter clearly has helped him get over the grief caused by her recent demise. Oh, she was so rich, and he is so glad she did not suffer through a long (and *expensive*) final illness. *Both of them are now in a much higher state of being.*

The attorney confirms the good news—your grandmother loved you. But then comes the bad news—in this jurisdiction (as in most states) *Grandma's letter of intent is not a will.* The crestfallen client barely hears the attorney describe what you have already learned. To be a will, the document must be signed in the presence of witnesses; the witnesses must observe that the testator has testamentary capacity and that no fraud, duress, or undue influence has been exerted on the testator; the witnesses must be told by the testator that this is the testator's will; the witnesses must be asked by the testator to witness the testator's signature; in addition to witnessing the testator's signature, the witnesses must witness each other signing as witnesses. Because Grandma's letter of intent has *none of these characteristics,* it is not and cannot be considered a will. Also, the distraught "heir" usually makes the futile and expensive attempt to convince a court that the letter of intent is indeed a will. May you never be left such a letter unless, of course, there is a will to back up your Granny's intentions.

Money-Saving Suggestions

If a legacy to a minor is not of great economic value, leave it to an adult and use a letter of intent to disclose your wishes. *This avoids the expense of a court supervision of the legacy until the child reaches adulthood.*

I also suggest that if you ever receive a letter of intent stating that you are to inherit everything, immediately tell the sender that the letter is appreciated. Then, strongly urge your well-intentioned benefactor to contact an attorney to learn about the document's legal limitations.

DIRECTIONS TO PAY DEBTS

The following is a typical clause in a will directing that the debts of the deceased are to be paid by the executor:

> I direct that all my *enforceable unsecured* debts, funeral expenses, the expenses of my last illness, and the administration expenses of my estate be paid by my executor as soon after my death as possible.

When using such a clause, here are two problems to avoid:

Do not use terms that may revive a debt you are no longer obliged to pay. An example is a debt that has been discharged in bankruptcy; another example is a debt that cannot be collected because the time when the creditor could bring a lawsuit has expired (this is called the expiration of the *statute of limitations*). Here is a debt-payment clause that might revive a bankruptcy debt or a debt barred by the statute of limitations: "I direct my Executor to pay all debts and claims *that are fair.*" Refrain from using such ambiguous language. In the typical clause, the adjective *enforceable* describes *debts,* thus preventing the revival of debts that have been extinguished by bankruptcy or the expiration of a statute of limitations.

Do not use words that could be construed to require payment of a debt secured by a mortgage. (As you probably know, a mortgage is a debt *secured* by real estate.) Suppose, for example, that a person dies at a time when his home has a mortgage balance of $80,000. Assume also that the home has been left to Mary. Is the $80,000 debt to be paid before Mary receives the home? No. However, if the debt-payment clause says that the executor must pay *all my debts,* Mary could argue that she is entitled to have the $80,000 debt paid, thereby receiving the home *without* a mortgage. In the typical clause, the adjective *unsecured* describes *debts,* thereby expressing the intention that the debt secured by the home is not to be paid by the executor. The sentence leaving the home to Mary should also specifically express your intention that the debt secured by the home is not to be paid by the estate; alternatively, if you want the debt paid off, then clearly state this intention.

Sample Situation

Whether or not your will states that debts are to be paid, believe me, they will be paid. Your creditors will not let the debt(s) be forgotten. But suppose the debts exceed assets. There is a priority in the payment of debts, and most states generally follow this order of payment: *secured claims,* family allowance, reasonable funeral expenses, necessary medical and hospital expenses of the last illness, costs and expenses of administering the estate, taxes, judgment debts, and then all other debts.

First on this above list are *secured claims.* A claim is secured if a court has on record that certain property is to be the source of payment of a particular debt. Examples include a mortgage on real property (which is land or a building) and a lien on personal property (which is everything else, e.g., cars, books, furniture, etc.). These secured claims are in a category by themselves because, generally, they are given a payment priority over other debts. They are *not subject to a proportional reduction where the total debts of the estate exceed the total assets of the estate.*

Here is an example of proportional reduction: Suppose the deceased left an estate consisting only of his home, valued at $50,000. Further suppose that the deceased's total debt was $100,000—owing $50,000 to a bank and $25,000 to each of two people. Therefore, the $50,000 in assets would pay only half the debts. The bank would receive $25,000, and each individual creditor would receive $12,500. However, if the bank had a mortgage (a secured claim) on the deceased's home, the bank would receive the full $50,000.

Money-Saving Suggestions

To the reader who may be a *creditor* of an estate, I stress the importance of bringing the debt—whether secured or unsecured—to the attention of the estate. Do this as soon as possible, and you should have an attorney represent you in your legal proceeding against an estate. A quick notification is important, because some states *allow only a short period of time* for creditors to present their claims. If you fail to act within this period of time, most likely the debt will not be paid.

To the reader who may be a *debtor,* I have this suggestion. If you have a favorite creditor, you might discuss with your attorney the possibility of giving this creditor a *security interest.* This way, the creditor receives priority over other creditors, either in the event of your bankruptcy or in the event of your death.

BURIAL DIRECTIONS

There is nothing wrong with having directions in your will that outline how you desire to be buried or how your physical remains are to be handled (e.g., cremation, donation for scientific purposes, or some special service). *But be sure that someone you trust is aware of these directions.* It is especially important that individuals who choose cremation express this desire not only in the will but also to a friend or relative who is likely to be in the position to carry out these wishes. Probably this friend or relative is the executor. The will might not be discovered *until after the family reconvenes from the burial at the cemetery.* So, to repeat, share your thoughts with a person close to you, and do it now. Incidentally, at one time religious teaching opposed cremation. This idea has been significantly modified, and few religions now oppose the practice.

At the time your will is drawn (better still, do it today), find out if there is a family *cemetery plot;* if so, who has the deed, and who is to be buried there. Families often find themselves searching for the deed when a relative dies. Usually the deed is located, but even if it cannot be found, the problem does eventually get resolved. The name of the cemetery is remembered, the cemetery finds its record of the plot location and identifies the owner, who then gives consent to the burial. But it is something that should not be left to the last minute; this is a time when family and friends should not be forced to undergo additional stress.

You may decide to have parts of your body used for *anatomical gifts,* or your entire body used for *medical research.* Eye banks, hospitals that perform organ transplants, and medical schools are frequently in need of these gifts. Many states have a section on driver's licenses where residents can express their desire to donate one or more body parts or their entire body for medical purposes.

Be sure to leave directions as to whether there is to be a traditional wake. Perhaps your preference is a *memorial service.* Opinion is mixed as to which of these offers the greater benefit to survivors. Some people are of the opinion that viewing the body is important, because it forces survivors to accept the death of a loved one. My preference is the memorial service, because the body is no longer as important as the type of life that was led. These are not pleasant thoughts, but if your survivors know your wishes, *the emotional stress on them can be significantly reduced.*

Sample Situation

You have the right to decide the manner in which your body is to be disposed. Put these instructions in your will and tell your decision to your executor (and perhaps another trusted person). When this has been done, you do not have to think further on the subject. At your death, the person to whom you have confided this information will follow your instructions.

Money-Saving Suggestions

To the person making the funeral arrangements, *be a smart shopper.* Never waste money; more importantly, never waste someone else's money! This someone else is the residuary legatee, whose legacy is decreased by the amount spent on the funeral (and who might advise the executor not to reimburse the person who orchestrated and paid for the lavish send-off of the deceased). Avoid the urge to go overboard; it is a meaningless effort to use a funeral to show the deceased the extent of your love. *If you are too confused or miserable to make wise choices, then ask someone to make these choices for you.*

Now a few words on planning for yourself. The least expensive alternative regarding body disposal is cremation with a memorial service. The expenses of embalming and renting a room in the funeral home are eliminated. Also there is no need for the purchase of an expensive casket or a gravestone. But it is your decision. *Whatever you decide, however, state your decision in your will and advise your executor accordingly.*

Suppose you change your mind after the will has been signed? *Do not make a change on your will.* Instead, have a new will drawn up or have a codicil prepared.

6

The Codicil

AMENDMENT TO A WILL

A *codicil* is an amendment to a will. Even though amended, the will remains valid; only those parts that are changed by the codicil are revoked. A codicil has the same requirement of legal formality as does a will: it must be *signed* and *dated;* the person must have testamentary capacity and must be signing the codicil *voluntarily;* the witnesses must be told that the document being signed is a codicil to a will and asked to witness the signature (as you know, this is *publication*); the codicil must be *witnessed* in the same manner as a will. A person's will, along with accompanying codicils, is presented to the court at the time of death.

I do not recommend a codicil, and my reasons are both procedural and substantive. It results in too many papers, too many affidavits, and possible confusion. When a codicil amends an earlier codicil, you then realize the problems of this shortcut. These are the *procedural reasons.*

An important *substantive* reason to avoid a codicil is the following. *Your will shows your intention before the codicil was executed.* Therefore, someone will clearly know that his or her legacy was diminished or eliminated by the codicil (just as someone will know that his or her legacy was enlarged by the codicil). *Why invite trouble for your estate from the person whose legacy was diminished?* That person may decide to challenge the codicil.

But even if a codicil is not an incentive to challenge, I still do not recommend it. If information serves no useful purpose, do not reveal it. Why let cousin Harry know that you had initially left him $10,000, but changed your mind and left $10,000 to cousin Susie instead? If you make this change with a *new will,* cousin Harry will probably never learn of the change. With a *codicil* cousin Harry knows he came close, but receives nothing. Even if he does not challenge the change, no purpose is served by letting him know what might have been?

Here is a quick question for you to consider. Recall that only the distributees can challenge a will. Who do you think is entitled to challenge a codicil? That's right—*the same distributees.* But now let me add something to your rapidly increasing knowledge: *Anyone whose legacy has been diminished by the codicil (or a later will) can challenge it.* For example, John, a friend of Mary, is bequeathed $40,000 through Mary's will. Her codicil eliminates his legacy. John, although not a distributee of Mary, can challenge her codicil.

Sample Situation

A few years ago, a client asked me to prepare a third codicil to his will. In this codicil was an amendment to the second codicil, an amendment to the first codicil, and an amendment to the original will. A new will turned out to be easier to prepare, and easier for my client to understand. Since then, I have prepared only a few first codicils, and I have not prepared any second codicils.

Money-Saving Suggestions

Tell your attorney to redraft the will rather than prepare a codicil, which is often confusing and no less expensive than redrafting an existing document. Many attorneys use word processors, so the typing task is now less burdensome. It is much easier for you to have your will contained in one document, instead of having numerous amendments. I repeat, the primary reason for having a new will prepared, rather than a codicil, is that a will *and* a codicil reveal too much. *The codicil antagonizes the person whose inheritance has been diminished by the change.*

If you feel that a codicil is the best approach for you, then *carefully* read your will and its codicil(s). Make sure the legal documents are clear to you; make sure they are not contradictory, and that there is no inconsistency between them; make sure each codicil is signed, dated, published, witnessed, and that the affidavit of the witnesses is obtained.

If your codicil was prepared for the purpose of leaving something to a charity, the following discussion in chapter 7 may offer some helpful advice, along with some useful suggestions.

7

Charities and Children

LEAVING A LITTLE SOMETHING TO CHARITY

If you have a favorite charity, perhaps you want to leave it something in your will. While there is no guarantee that such philanthropy will secure a place for you in heaven, what you leave to a charity brightens the lives of other people.

Some states impose a *limitation* on how much can be left to a charity. There might be a law that does not allow an amount over a specific percentage of your assets to be left to a charity; however, the law is perhaps applicable only if there is a surviving spouse or a surviving child to protect. Most states, however, do allow you to leave everything to a charity. But, again, perhaps there is an exception, such as: if you leave everything (or even something) to a charity and *die shortly thereafter.* The charity might be prohibited from receiving this legacy (or the court might inquire as to whether any undue influence was exerted on the testator).

Your attorney can advise you on any particular limitation that your state imposes upon charitable legacies, but here are some further thoughts on charities that are applicable *everywhere:*

Make sure that you clearly identify the charity. Write to the charity and request its *legal name.*

What happens if at your death the charity named in your will *is not in existence?* Perhaps a *successor charity* should be named in the event that this happens.

Charities must meet various state and federal requirements to remain tax exempt. But suppose at your death the charity is no longer a qualified charity as determined by the Internal Revenue Service. Since contributions only to a qualified charity are allowable as tax deductions, perhaps a successor charity should be named in your will in the event this happens (so that your estate receives a tax deduction for the amount of this legacy).

Be alert in choosing your favorite charity. There are some wonderful organizations, and some not so wonderful ones. Familiarize yourself with the leadership, finances, purposes, and effectiveness of your chosen charity.

Sample Situations

A major source of funding for most charities consists of legacies in the wills of generous benefactors. If you decide to leave money, stocks, bonds, etc., to a charity, give the organization *discretion regarding how to use the legacy.* If you follow this suggestion, the words "for its general purposes" should be included, along with the name of the charity and the amount of the legacy. This helps the organization in two ways: it gives the charity flexibility and it reduces the charity's bookkeeping chore.

Allowing a charity to use the legacy for its general purposes avoids the following problem. Suppose a legacy is limited to a particular purpose, and the purpose is obsolete at the time the charity is to receive the legacy. A case that comes to mind is the gift of money to a medical charity, but the legacy is limited to *research on a specific disease.* Suppose the disease is already eliminated (cured) by the time the benefactor dies. The broader directive "for its general purposes" may be more appropriate.

Another case where the stated particular purpose of a legacy can become a problem is when the gift is intended for the construction of a *new building.* Suppose the charity does not need a new building at the time of your death? Again, I suggest the broader directive "for its general purposes."

Here is an alternative approach: Again, suppose you want the charity to use the money for scientific research on a specific disease (or for the construction of a new building, etc.). State this purpose but add a clause that *if this purpose is not feasible, the charity may use this money for its general purposes.*

Money-Saving Suggestions

If you want your estate to obtain a charitable tax deduction, you are required to *leave the legacy to the entire charity and not just to a specific division.* For example, your estate could have a problem if you chose to leave a legacy to *the library* of ABC Charity, because the library is neither a legal entity nor a charity. You should state your intention: "I leave this legacy to ABC Charity, to be used, if possible, for its library; otherwise, the legacy is to be used by ABC Charity for its general purposes."

As for choosing a charity, I suggest this approach. *Volunteer to do some work for the charity.* This is a great way to learn about the organization, to help others, and to help yourself. You will receive that wonderful feeling of accomplishment when you make a meaningful contribution to those who truly need it. If you have questions about charities, contact your state attorney general's office for information pertaining to investigations of fraud.

CHILDREN

The loss of a parent is painful, but being disinherited is also painful. If the child believes the exclusion from a parent's will is the result of a loosely worded document, this can be devastating. Make your intentions clear if you have (or acquire) a child. A child can be legally classified in a variety of ways:

the *traditional* child, resulting from the union of a married man and woman or a marriage-like relationship (e.g., common law marriage);

the *adopted* child, whose legal status has been confirmed by an adoption proceeding;

the *stepchild,* whose parent has remarried and the new spouse has not legally adopted the child;

the *surrogate* child, born to a mother who, before the nonsexual conception occurred, relinquished custody of the child to the biological father;

the *out-of-wedlock* child, also called a biological child, whose parents brought it into the world in a traditional manner, but the father and mother were not married when the child was born;

the *posthumous* child, born after the father's death; and

the *after-born* child, also called the pretermitted child, who is born after the parent signed a will.

This last category, the child born to the testator after the will is written, is protected by statute in many states. This child can also be protected by stating *in your will* what legacy (if any) is to be received by a child, *of whatever type,* who comes into your life after you sign your will. You can also have a new will prepared after the arrival of a child.

This subject of identifying various categories of children is important to older persons, even if the elderly leave everything to their adult children. Successor legatees might be grandchildren (in the event that the older person is predeceased by his or her children). For example, if your son predeceases you, do you want his adopted child to share your estate? Whether you do or not, spell it out.

Sample Situation

With your will there is an element of suspense; until the time of your death, perhaps only you and your attorney know for sure what has been set forth in the document and how your wishes are to be carried out. Two dramatic changes are taking place in our society: there is a *breakdown of the family structure,* and people are *living longer.* I have no idea if these two changes are interrelated, but I do know that these changes have resulted in children being disinherited. Families are scattered all over the United States, if not the world. With increased longevity, this separation of parents from their children can often be a long one. The parents may be far away, emotionally as well as geographically; they may have established new friends and new lives. The cases are numerous where children are not left a legacy by either the first parent to die or the second. *Again, there is nothing wrong in disinheriting a child.* But most elders do leave their fortunes to their children. However, *you are in control regarding this matter,* so make up your own mind.

Money-Saving Suggestions

Whether you plan to disinherit or to leave a legacy to a child, make sure you clearly identify both your *intent* as well as the *identity* of the child(ren). If you are leaving something to a child who is adopted, state the name of your child. If you have another child, or adopt a child, or marry someone with a child, take the time to read your will; perhaps you might want to speak to your attorney to learn if your current will provides for this new child. *If you so desire, have a provision in your will to address the possibility of a child who might be born or adopted after you have executed the document.*

If you are leaving something to your friend, and you direct that if this friend predeceases you then the legacy goes to your friend's children, be sure to state the name(s) of the child(ren); you might even want to add the following clause to protect any after-born or adopted children: "and to any other children who are born or adopted."

NAMING A GUARDIAN

It is important for a parent (or perhaps a grandparent who has legal custody) of a young child to plan for the possibility that the child will be an orphan. You can appoint in your will the person who will be legally responsible for your child. This person is called a *guardian.*

In Part Four of this volume, I will discuss topics similar to that of "guardian": namely, *conservators* and *committees.* The conservator is an individual who is appointed by a court to manage an adult's property (which, of course, includes money). A committee is an individual appointed by a court and entrusted with the total care of the adult—*both the person and his or her property.* The concept of a guardian is discussed here in Part One because, unlike a conservator or a committee, *the guardian of a minor is appointed through a will.*

You must decide who is best qualified to take care of the child in the event of your death, and then ask yourself whether the person would be willing to assume this responsibility. If you think this qualified person would be willing, approach the person with your proposal. If the person expresses a willingness, then *name this person in your will* as the guardian. Consider having an alternate guardian named in your will, in case your first choice is unavailable or unwilling, if the need arises, to serve as guardian. Here is a sample clause appointing a guardian:

If my spouse, (give name), predeceases me, and any child of mine is under the age of majority at my death, or if my spouse survives me and dies, while any child of mine is under the age of majority, without having nominated a guardian of each child of mine, I hereby nominate, constitute, and appoint my friend (give name), currently residing at (give address), as the guardian of each child of mine. If this person for any reason, shall fail to qualify or cease to act as such guardian, I hereby nominate, constitute and appoint my friend (give name), currently residing at (give address), as successor guardian. I expressly direct that no bond or security of any kind shall be required of any guardian in any jurisdiction to secure the faithful performance of duties and, to the extent legally permissible, I hereby relieve the guardian from filing accounts of the guardianship in any court.

The real benefit to naming a guardian in your will is the *planning that accompanies your choice.* The fact that the person you selected has expressed a willingness to serve is also a benefit.

Sample Situations

Whenever there is placement of a child—whether into a foster home, an adoptive home, with one of the divorced parents, or with a guardian after the child has been orphaned—the court usually interviews the child. Sometimes the child is also interviewed by social workers and psychiatrists.

I vividly remember a case in which I expressed to the court one of the relevant factors on child placement—*the wishes of the nine-year-old child.* The judge indignantly responded that the decision in the case should not be made by a nine-year-old. Although the child should not decide with whom placement is to be entrusted, in my opinion *the child's wishes surely should be considered.* In selecting the appropriate guardian, listen to what the child says about the person you plan to appoint as guardian and include this input with your own ideas.

Money-Saving Suggestion

Consider entrusting the legacy you leave your child to a person *other than* the child's guardian. Perhaps your sister could be the person entrusted with your child's legacy, and you would name her as *guardian of the child's property.* At periodic intervals she could provide money to your brother, who could be the *guardian of your child.* This way you have an extra pair of eyes watching your child and your child's money. Of course, if you are thinking of choosing different people for these separate roles, consider whether they get along with each other. One other point: you do not have to choose a family member to be the guardian.

I have already suggested that you listen to the opinion of the person for whom a guardian is to be appointed. Some people, however, are hesitant to discuss death, especially their own. I agree, there should be a hesitancy. *Death is difficult to contemplate, whether you are nine or ninety.* However, the subject of death can and should be discussed, but with an awareness that the possibility of the loss of a loved one—especially when there is a reliance upon this loved one—is a frightening concept to everyone.

Planning for the future of your potential orphan or your elderly parent avoids two extreme situations. There is the survivor who is *loved too much;* ironically, family members fight to show their love. The other extreme is the *unloved survivor,* who gets bounced from family to family because no one wants to assume this responsibility.

Now that you have taken the time to plan for the well-being of people in your care, it's time once more to consider the most important person in your will—you.

8

Some Final Thoughts

YOUR INVENTORY

I have already suggested the need for an inventory, a simple list, of what you own. Here are three reasons for having an inventory: it makes your life more *orderly,* it makes your *financial assets more understandable,* and it makes your *survivors' job easier.* But I really want you to have an inventory *in order to prevent your state government from receiving your assets.*

My concern is not so much with your household items (although you should have a list of the contents of your home and give a copy of it to your home insurance agent), but with your *money assets.* Assets that are owned by you at the time of your death—but unknown to your executor and therefore never collected and distributed to your legatees—will be turned over to the state as property that has been abandoned by the owner. If you want your assets distributed to those you love, then you *must let your executor know what you own through your inventory.* I also advise married couples to review their asset inventory; both parties should know and understand their combined finances. There are too many unfortunate situations where the surviving spouse does not know the total assets owned by the deceased spouse.

With the proliferation of certificates of deposit (CDs), tax-deferred investments, tax-exempt investments, zero-coupon bonds, mutual funds, Individual Retirement Accounts (IRAs), and so on, it is possible that you will lose—or your executor will never locate—one or more of your investments. Look at the long lists of names that local banks periodically publish in newspapers. The lists contain names of depositors whose accounts have

66

been inactive for a number of years, and the banks are attempting to locate the holders of these accounts. It is a fact that many of these depositors are dead. It is also a fact that *the money in these accounts will eventually be owned by the state government if the funds go unclaimed.* The legal term describing this transfer of abandoned assets to the state is *escheat.*

At the time your will is drafted, make an *inventory* of all your assets. For your bank accounts, include the account number along with the address of the bank; for your shares of corporate stock, include the name of your stockbroker if these shares of corporate stock are held in a brokerage account. Update your list annually; your list does not have to be typed. Each year you can just cross out those assets you no longer own and add the new assets. A convenient time for the annual update is after the April 15th filing of your income tax return. Your attorney should see this inventory, and *your executor should know where your inventory is located.* Your insurance broker should be consulted as to whether all the items on your list are adequately insured.

I cannot emphasize enough the need for this inventory; bank accounts and other financial accounts do get lost—in some cases forever. Elderly citizens are at particular risk because other problems, such as illness, might distract them from keeping their financial affairs in order.

Sample Situation

Estates frequently have this significant problem: difficulty in discovering what the deceased owned. This problem can be easily prevented.

Schedule B from your federal individual income tax return is a good starting point for your inventory. This schedule lists all your taxable interest and dividends. I advise clients to ask their tax preparer to list the account number after the source of the income: for example, ABC Bank, Account Number 01–117,003. Photocopy this schedule and you have most of your financial inventory completed.

Not only is this an easy way to prepare your inventory, but it also helps if an income tax audit occurs. If the Internal Revenue Service's computer beeps when it scans your return, perhaps the account number will clarify the situation when a human being examines your return. If it does not clarify the situation, you may be required to meet with an Internal Revenue Service auditor. At this stage of the audit, your records can save you dollars that otherwise might be assessed by the tax auditor.

Money-Saving Suggestion

You, not just your heirs, benefit from this list of assets. You may learn that *some investments are doing better than others,* and you may decide to make some investment changes. For example, make a comparison between *the after-tax money in your pocket from taxable income and the money in your pocket from tax-exempt income.* A tax-exempt income yield of eight percent interest is better than a taxable income yield of ten percent interest for those in the higher income bracket who are taxed at a twenty-eight percent rate. The inventory therefore becomes far more than a list; it comprises many facts that can be used to evaluate your investments. The inventory makes your life more *organized.*

LIBEL AND PROVISIONS AGAINST PUBLIC POLICY

The existence in a will of *a provision that is offensive to someone may be the source of a lawsuit.* The offended person could prevail in a suit based on *libel,* a legal action for damage done to a person's reputation.

As I mentioned earlier, try not to be humorous or sarcastic in describing someone in your will. Most definitely, do not have your will become the foundation for a libel lawsuit. Refrain from describing someone as a thieving scoundrel. While some courts might say that the scoundrel in question has no action against your estate, other courts might well hold your estate liable for the injury that your will has inflicted on this *thieving scoundrel's reputation.* Resist the urge to have the last word, because, in the end, the person you libel may get your last penny.

Another reason for urging you to refrain from writing humorous or nasty words in your will is the concept of *testamentary capacity,* a fundamental feature of any valid will. If you attack someone in your will, the opportunity presents itself for the injured party to question your state of mind when you signed the will. It would be ironic if the final consequence of those well-placed nasty words is a court determination that you lacked testamentary capacity.

A situation similar to the libelous statement is that known as the *provision against public policy.* For example, a father leaves his daughter the whole of his estate, but imposes a condition that *first she must get divorced.* This is a provision against public policy and will not be enforced. This subject is further discussed in the next sample situation.

Sample Situation

Just as the law does not permit you to use your will as an instrument to destroy a person's character or reputation, *a provision in your will that is against public policy will not be recognized by the court.* There are cases of a legacy being left to an individual, but only if that individual does something. If the required action is against public policy, the court can *disregard the provision.* The example above is a case in point: a legacy to a person is conditioned on the provision that the person *must get divorced* before the legacy can be received.

One case where the legacy was conditioned on the provision that the person *must get married* supposedly can be found in the will of George Bernard Shaw. The story is told that he intended to leave everything to his wife on the condition that she remarry within one year after his death. He wanted to be sure at least one person would grieve his passing.

Do not have this type of provision in your will. After the laughter subsides, your will may be denied probate, or the legatee may not get the legacy, or the legatee may get the legacy without the provision being enforced. The provision is, at best, *meaningless;* at worst, it *denies all your legatees their legacies.*

Money-Saving Suggestions

Neither libel someone in your will nor impose a condition on a legacy that is against public policy. Your will is a serious legal document. Its purpose is to distribute your assets to those whom you wish to receive them. This purpose can be defeated if you write your will in a frivolous fashion; your estate will also incur unnecessary legal fees.

Here is a practical suggestion. Why wait until you are dead to tell a person how upset you are about something the individual said or did? Tell the person now; you might be pleasantly surprised at the result. Even if the problem remains unresolved, you have had the satisfaction of expressing your displeasure.

A LIVING WILL

A *living will* is a document outlining how a person wants to be medically treated in the event of a terminal illness or a condition that requires decisions about the use of life-sustaining procedures. If the person is later rendered *unable to communicate a medical treatment decision,* then the desires expressed in the living will are what society is asked to recognize.

The living will is used by an individual who does not want to be subjected to a futile prolongation of the dying process. Your living will can state a desire that life support systems, feeding tubes, and heroic measures are not to be used when there is no chance of recovery. It is not the expression of a desire to end life; it is an appeal that medical technology not be used to *prolong the dying process if no reasonable chance of recovery is likely.*

The living will is an assertion of a person's right to *self-determination.* Some people are in favor of it as an expression of personal autonomy and thus conclude that it is a means to *allow* death to take place. Others, most particularly those opposed to the living will, are of the mind that it is a means to *cause* death. What do you think? Here is a wallet-size summary of the living will:

TO MY FAMILY, PHYSICIAN, AND HOSPITAL: If there is no reasonable expectation of my recovery from extreme physical or mental disability, I direct that I be allowed to die and not be kept alive by artificial means and heroic measures. I ask that medication be mercifully administered to me for terminal suffering even though this may shorten my life.

I hope that you who care for me will feel morally bound to act in accordance with this urgent request. *(This wallet-size summary is distributed by the organization called Concern for Dying.)*

After you sign your living will, it is signed by witnesses. Suggested witnesses are your doctor, attorney, or executor, although any competent person can be a witness.

Sample Situation

All of us have read in the newspaper or seen on television the story of the terminally ill comatose patient kept alive by so-called heroic measures. In many of these cases there is confusion among those who love the person. The question is repeated: "What does my sick friend want?" A living will provides the answer; it helps both you and those you love in times of great despair. The vast majority of states now recognize the living will.

A real benefit of the living will is that your family, attorney, executor, doctor, and hospital know your thoughts and wishes on the subject of heroic medical treatment. But most importantly, your acceptance or rejection of the living will *forces you to reach a decision regarding extraordinary medical procedures.* Make up your mind on this subject and let your wishes be known. Have a living will prepared if you want to exercise this self-determination.

Money-Saving Suggestions

Unnecessary, unwanted, painful, and expensive medical treatment may be eliminated by signing a living will. If you have a living will, make sure that your *doctor* is aware of it and insist that the document be shown to any *hospital* that ever admits you as a patient. (To receive more information on the living will, write to Choice in Dying, 200 Varick Street, New York, New York 10014-4810. This organization and its predecessor organizations have distributed millions of copies of the living will since 1967.)

Here is another suggestion: If you have a problem distinguishing between a living will and euthanasia, discuss this subject with someone. Perhaps your doctor, minister (rabbi or priest), or attorney can provide some direction. Although they can help you prepare to reach your decision, they cannot make these choices for you. *It is your responsibility to decide what is best for you.*

Allow me to give you my rebuttal to one of the arguments against a living will. The argument is that the doctor might withhold treatment in a case where the patient *clearly has a chance of recovery.* My answer: in this hypothetical case the doctor is incompetent; seeking a second opinion, not the rejection of a living will, is how to *limit the possibility of a medical mistake.*

UPDATING A WILL

If you decide to change your will, see your attorney and have a new one prepared. Remember that the will is dated; the document with the most recent date is your *last will and testament.* What should you do with your old will? Save it, because it serves as a good record of your desires over the years. Your attorney should be the one to save it, so that the prior wills are not available after your death to the casual observer of your personal papers. Here are some thoughts on when a will should be updated:

when your wealth increases: perhaps as a result of having received a legacy;

when you get married, become a parent (or a grandparent), or get divorced;

when a person named in your will dies, and you have changed your mind about the successor named to receive the legacy;

when any person named in your will falls out of your favor;

when a legatee becomes profligate and you want to leave the legacy in a trust to protect the wealth from being improperly spent;

when your opinion of your executor changes; and

when you become aware of an estate tax law change.

The cost of a legal consultation or preparing a new will is far less than the amount that can be saved by sound planning.

Do not make any changes to your existing will without consulting your attorney. Suppose you cross out something in a will. What you might have done is destroy the whole will; in some states you have done nothing, that is, the part you thought you deleted remains as part of the will. If a court has to determine the legal effect of your crossing out, this future cost to your estate will significantly exceed the present cost to you for preparation of a new will. *To change your will requires either a new will or a codicil. In either case, the legal formalities (witnessing, etc.) are the same.* Also, remember what you have learned about codicils. I do not recommend this shortcut; have a new will prepared and it should be no more expensive than the amendment you contemplated.

Sample Situations

Generally, the law considers your will to have been revoked if you destroy the document. Furthermore, the law presumes that a missing will was destroyed *by you,* the testator, if it was in your possession and cannot be found. "Presumes" here means what is accepted as fact, unless contradictory evidence is provided. So, if you *accidentally* lose the original of your will, upon your death the law considers your will to have been revoked by you, *unless proven otherwise. To prove otherwise is difficult,* because your executor (who will bear this burden of proof) will not know whether you ripped it up *deliberately* or threw it out *accidentally.*

Here is another reason *not* to keep your original will at home. After your death, someone not named in the will might be the person who discovers the existence of the will and then destroys it. Therefore, you might want to consider having someone safeguard this important document.

Should your attorney hold the original will while you retain a copy? It might be safer to proceed in this fashion. But be aware that some attorneys desire to hold the original of the will in order to increase the chance of eventually *representing the executor of your estate.* This presumes that the executor will hire the attorney who prepared and safeguarded the will (and also presumes that the attorney will outlive the testator). Both presumptions are speculative and perhaps not all that significant, but there is no harm in sharing these ideas with you. If the attorney who holds your will happens to die before you do, then contact the attorney's office (frequently the law office will contact all of the attorney's clients in such cases) and either retrieve the will or select some other attorney in the firm to be the person responsible for safeguarding your last will and testament.

Two other places to keep your original will are: (1) with your executor (or some other trusted person) or (2) in your safe deposit box. However, if the latter option is used, be sure that directions contained in the original will pertaining to such matters as your burial have been unequivocally stated by you to your most trusted person (probably your executor), who in this instance should be in possession of a copy of the will. Your executor should have no problem gaining access to your safe deposit box at the time of your death.

Money-Saving Suggestion

While I believe attorneys are necessary in preparing wills, do not become what I refer to as a *will groupie.* This is a person overly preoccupied by the will, and who pays unnecessary attorney's fees. Some people do this because they enjoy talking with the attorney about who is getting what, who is not getting what, and how their legatees (and nonlegatees) may react. A tip-off on whether you are a will groupie is if you are overly concerned about the *reading of the will.* Remember that there is no such thing. A will that is carefully prepared by your attorney should not have to be changed more than a few times in your lifetime. Perhaps your will can last for your entire life. *But take a look at your will each year at about tax time,* perhaps when you update your inventory of assets. If there has been a significant change in your life, then go see an attorney.

AN ATTORNEY IS NECESSARY

Yes, an attorney *is necessary* to advise you on every area covered in this book. But do not hire the first attorney you interview; comparative shopping is a good way to educate yourself. Listed below is a four-step approach to your first encounter with an attorney. Discuss *experience, speed, outcome,* and *fee,* as follows:

> Ask questions about the attorney's *experience* with the particular legal matter. Spend time getting to know the attorney; allow this person to get to know you.
>
> Ask *how long* it is going to take the attorney to solve your problem. An attorney who does this for a living should know the answer.
>
> Obtain the attorney's prediction on the *outcome* of the legal problem. Perhaps you will learn that the attorney *cannot* solve your problem.
>
> Discuss the *fee.* The attorney may not be able to give an exact fee, but you should at least receive a clear estimate of the approximate amount to be charged. Learn how the attorney has calculated this amount. Is it based on the size of the estate? Is it based on the estimated number of hours of work? Also, you should know at what time payment is due. If you hire the attorney, have this fee agreement clearly stated in a follow-up letter (written either by you or the attorney). The disbursement costs, such as court filing fees and other expenses, also should be explained to you.

In summary, whether you are dealing with an attorney, a doctor, an automobile mechanic, or a plumber, you should ask about the *experience* of the person providing the service, *how long* it will take, what is the anticipated *outcome,* and what is the *fee.*

Shakespeare wrote that *all attorneys should be killed.* Try these more moderate alternatives: when you need an attorney, hire one; but before you hire an attorney, be careful and *ask questions.* If the relationship becomes unsatisfactory to you, *put an end to it (the relationship, not the attorney's life).*

Sample Situations

Some people consider attorneys to be rascals, while others see them as heroes. Perhaps it started when Aaron represented Moses before the pharaoh and *lost his case*. Perhaps it started when Thomas More represented the pope before King Henry and *lost his case*. Most attorneys are neither heroes nor rascals. *They are people providing a service on a subject matter known to them.* Sometimes they win, sometimes they lose, and sometimes *the distinction between victory and defeat is somewhat unclear.*

A mistaken view is that attorneys are *all-powerful*. Not true. Attorneys are like *jockeys:* they provide direction within defined boundaries, guide the matter to a conclusion, and try to have the results pay off for the client. Perhaps a perfect solution to the legal problem does not exist and compromise is the alternative. Most troublesome, however, are the cases in which the attorney does not advise the client at the outset of what can and cannot be achieved. The client has high expectations; the attorney hesitates to be the bearer of bad news; and when the client's expectations are not realized, the client justifiably feels that the attorney did not perform satisfactorily.

A final observation is that attorneys are not *psychiatrists*. Particularly with family problems, your attorney should not be expected to solve the nonlegal aspects of these disputes. Your legal counsel, however, can give guidance as to how you can solve the problems, or at least he can listen as you articulate and clarify the problems. Conversely, *if the attorney increases the family's problems, then hire another lawyer.*

Money-Saving Suggestions

Good legal advice can save a substantial amount of money. You should hire an attorney to plan your estate and to advise you on those few major legal decisions that confront each of us. We have all heard stories about the terrible attorney (doctor, auto mechanic, plumber). *If you have a problem with an attorney, then hire a more qualified legal counsel.*

Here is some advice that is simple but often disregarded: *good communication* solves a lot of problems. Your relationship with your attorney should be a close one, so talk with your lawyer.

THE ATTORNEY'S JOB

Words that have a specific legal meaning should be used only if both you and your attorney understand them. Helping you to understand in a general way every *word*, every *sentence*, and every *paragraph* in your will is one of your attorney's most important jobs. Your attorney's function also includes:

Helping you understand what you own. This might require an appraisal of your business, an explanation of the death benefits available from your employer, an evaluation of your life insurance, or confirmation of your ownership interest in a particular parcel of real estate.

Advising you on estate taxes that might be owed by your estate and suggesting ways to lessen them.

Listening patiently and asking you to express your thoughts and feelings as to why someone should or should not be in your will. This is the extent of the direction the attorney should give in responding to the question, "Do you think I should leave her anything?"

Assisting you in the preparation of a will.

Assuring you that your will conforms to the laws of your state.

Giving you advice on related subjects, such as: medicare and medicaid, private health insurance, social security, the income tax treatment of any lump-sum pension distributions, and addressing all the legal issues now confronting you or eventually confronting your estate. Perhaps the best job the attorney can perform in some of these areas is to refer you to an attorney who specializes in the particular subject of concern.

The relationship between an attorney and a client is a close one, especially in this area of will preparation. *Be candid with your attorney.* What you tell your attorney is held in confidence. The attorney cannot repeat information to anyone without your consent.

Sample Situation

Real property includes land and buildings; everything else is *personal property.* Therefore, your *shares of stock,* your car, your furniture, your jewelry, your clothing, and your bankbooks are all *personal property.* Suppose your will directs that someone is to receive *all your personal property.* You now know that any shares of stock you own in General Motors Corporation, in your cooperative apartment, or in your family-owned corporation will go to this person receiving *all your personal property.* It is your attorney's job to advise you on the importance of every word in your will, *particularly if the word has a legal meaning.* Otherwise, your will might be expressing something contrary to your wishes.

Money-Saving Suggestion

Be safe, spell out the items you intend to leave to various people. Do not rely on confusing general terms such as *personal property, tangible personal property,* and *personal effects.* These expressions may sound similar, but they have entirely different meanings.

Personal property is a broad category and includes everything other than land and buildings. As explained in the sample situation, it includes shares of stock in a corporation.

Tangible personal property distinguishes tangible items, which are items that can be felt (an example is your jewelry), from things that are symbolic of something (an example is your bankbook, which is symbolic of the money in the account). So the person receiving your tangible personal property will receive your jewelry but not your bankbook.

Personal effects means your clothing and other items that are closely connected with you. Obviously this definition is quite vague. Does it include your pants? Yes. Does it include your wallet? Yes. Does it include the money in your wallet? No. Does it include the contents of a safe deposit box if the key to the box is in your wallet? No.

GUILT, GREED, EXPLOITATION, AND UNDUE INFLUENCE

Oh, what emotions a will stirs! If a friend or relative asks your advice on whether a will is necessary, say yes. I have heard many people recount a tale similar to the following:

> My ninety-six-year-old aunt said, "I think I should put my affairs in order, please help me." So as not to appear greedy, I responded, "Oh, there's no rush, *you're not going to die."*

The person asking for your advice is most likely thinking of leaving you money, appointing you as executor, or both. *You can help that person and also help yourself.* Do not feel guilty, greedy, unworthy, or anything of the kind. On the other hand, do not let that person exploit you. Do not bank on the promise that *you are in my will.* Maybe you are the potential legatee; but there is also the possibility that you are being exploited.

Remember reading about undue influence? You learned that a person's will must not be the result of undue influence having been exerted. However, *good salesmanship is not undue influence.* But those who can talk a person into leaving them some money are unique indeed. My experience is that people can see through the various ploys and cajolings, and are offended by someone asking for a legacy. The request for a legacy usually results not only in a strained relationship but in no legacy. *Suggest the importance of a will;* this is the best salesmanship.

Most individuals die without a will, and thus do not exercise their right to choose who receives their property, however large or small it may be. We are complex creatures: our lives, our relationships, our finances, and the reasons some give for having wills (and others for not having them) are probably just as complicated. It is my opinion, however, that *a person without a will is a person who avoids thoughts of death,* those vague thoughts of nothingness, of being a flicker in the galaxy, of judgment, of perfect happiness. Whether or not you think about it, however, death is inevitable. But your will, unlike your death, is something within your control. So think about your will, plan your estate, and stop thinking about death, and . . . *thy will be done.*

Sample Situations

The cases of disappointed heirs are sad stories. These people were told they would get the booty. Perhaps they were told the truth, but a later will then knocked them out. Or perhaps they were being fooled, and learned the sad truth upon the death of the person who lied to them. Another case that frequently occurs is the rich relative who honestly alerts the legatees of their potential good fortune, but the high cost of medical care, perhaps nursing home care, *depletes the assets of this relative who had once been rich.*

Do not exploit others, and do not let anyone exploit you. It serves no purpose to tell someone that there is a legacy for them in the future. *Most people do not reveal the names of the legatees. This is what I advise.* Although you should not tell your legatees that they are in your will, I again advise you to *ask* your executor if he or she will serve in that capacity. I suggest this for the following reasons: Not only is it a courtesy that should be extended to the potential executor, it gives you the opportunity to tell this person where your will and asset inventory are kept. Most importantly, it is the only way to find out if the person is willing to serve as your executor.

Money-Saving Suggestion

Some people feel uncomfortable when told by a friend or relative that they are named in the will. I repeat, do not feel guilty, greedy, unworthy, or obligated to act differently toward your potential benefactor. Continue the same relationship you enjoyed before you were informed. *This suggestion can save you the energy and expense of caring for someone who is exploiting you.* Ask yourself if you would otherwise render this care. Do not think that if you help someone, then you will be rewarded with a legacy. There are legions of disappointed people who mistakenly believed they were the heirs apparent. Keep in mind, care and concern should be *motivated by love, not by money.*

A LIVING (INTER VIVOS) TRUST

No treatment of wills is complete without a discussion of trusts. This section on a living trust introduces the subject. *Testamentary trusts* are discussed in the next section.

A *trust* is a contract between a person and a trustee, whereby the person transfers money or other property to the trustee, who holds the property for the benefit of someone else. There are three parties involved: the person with the money is called the *settlor* (or the *grantor*); the person entrusted with possession of the money is called the *trustee;* and the person benefiting from the money is called the *beneficiary.*

An *inter vivos* trust is made by a *living person.* (Incidentally, *inter vivos* is Latin for "between the living," and most people refer to this type of trust as a *living trust.*) A *testamentary trust* is the same as a living trust, except that the trust is established *in a person's will,* and it thus takes effect upon the person's death.

A trust agreement, like any contract, gives you flexibility as to what terms and conditions are agreed to by the settlor and the trustee. For example, the settlor can require the trustee to give the income annually to the beneficiary, or the settlor can require that the trustee accumulate the income and delay giving any money to the beneficiary until a later time. The settlor can establish guidelines as to how the trustee is to invest the trust funds, specify when the trustee is to terminate the trust, and direct how the trustee is to distribute the balance of the trust funds when the trust is terminated.

The settlor, by appointing someone to control the money, is exerting a control over the beneficiary. When you think of a trust, whether a living trust or a testamentary one, think of *control.*

One trust provision I favor is called a *sprinkling income provision.* It gives the trustee the power to distribute income among a few beneficiaries, and not necessarily in equal shares. From year to year the trustee can decide which beneficiary (or beneficiaries), is (are) to receive the income. The trustee can also decide the amount of income that is to be received by each beneficiary.

Sample Situation

A client once asked me why living trusts are used in cases where a lot of money is involved. Administrative and legal costs make trusts impractical for the less well-off person. If the individual setting up the trust is not well off, the tax savings are small or nonexistent. You will learn more about tax savings in Part Three, but let us take a quick look at taxes right now.

Money-Saving Suggestion

Income tax savings and *estate tax savings* can result from the use of a living trust.

Suppose mother puts $10,000 into a living trust for the benefit of her twenty-year-old son. *Income tax savings* are realized, assuming that the yield (the interest income) from the money is likely to be taxed at a lower rate for the son, rather than at the possibly higher rate the mother might be required to pay on similar income. The *estate tax savings* arises because she has reduced her taxable estate by at least a portion of the amount of the trust. In addition, there is the estate tax savings on the amount which the $10,000 might have increased over the remainder of the mother's life.

However, savings on income and estate taxes would have resulted even if she had given the money *outright to the son.* But a trust has the *additional* tax benefit of keeping this money *out of the son's eventual estate,* as we will see by once again looking at this example of a living trust:

Wealthy Mother delivers $10,000 to the ABC Trust Company. It is to be held in trust for her son. Mother is the *settlor;* ABC Trust Company is the *trustee;* the son is the *beneficiary.* The trust company is to invest the money and distribute the income annually to the son. Upon the son's death, the trust company is to end the trust and *distribute the principal in the trust to her other children surviving her son. The principal in this trust is not included in the taxable estate of the son.*

The mother can decide to give the trustee discretion to distribute some of the *principal* (the $10,000) to the son at whatever time the trustee so decides. She also can decide to have the trustee retain the income until the son reaches a certain age, and then start to make distributions to him. There are practically no limits on the terms the mother can include in the trust.

A TRUST IN THE WILL (TESTAMENTARY TRUST)

A testamentary trust is the same as a living trust, except *it is contained in a will and takes effect when the testator dies.* It is a way to leave a legacy to someone and at the same time *control* the timing of the distribution to the legatee. Furthermore, it is a way to *control* where that legacy will go when the legatee dies. You might want to establish a testamentary trust in these situations:

money is left to a *minor child;*

money is left to a profligate adult who is likely to *squander* it if the legacy is not protected;

money is left to an adult who is unable to *manage* it;

money is left to someone who is *mentally incompetent;*

you want to exert *control* over the funds for a period of time (i.e., you want to exert control over the person's use of the money for that person's lifetime, and upon that person's death you want to exert control over the choice of the eventual recipient of the money—in which case, your trustee is your *controlling hand from the grave*); or

you want the *estate of the person receiving your money to avoid future estate taxes* (and my next money-saving suggestion explains this idea).

A trust, whether *living* or *testamentary,* offers you flexibility; your attorney can custom prepare it to fulfill your wishes. *The power of the trustee can be extensive or quite limited.* I caution you to avoid being too rigid or too vague in your directions to the trustee.

One example of being *too rigid* would be an absolute direction to the trustee that the trust principal always consist of fifty percent stock and fifty percent tax-exempt bonds. This instruction would have an ironic result. When the stock comprising fifty percent of the trust principal is doing poorly and decreases in value, some of the tax-exempt bonds would have to be sold to buy more stock to maintain the equal value of stocks and tax-exempt bonds in the trust.

An example of being *too vague* is an absolute direction to the trustee that the trust principal is never to be invested in companies that are *antisocial.* Would this vague standard allow a trustee to invest in a company that makes military equipment? Could the trustee invest in a company that produces food high in cholesterol?

Try to strike a balance between *rigid instructions* and *vague instructions* to the trustee.

Sample Situation

As with *living* trusts, *testamentary* trusts are generally used only by the wealthy. That is, the person establishing the trust is wealthy; the beneficiary may or may not be. Can the beneficiary, who but for the trust is poor, qualify for social welfare benefits such as medicaid? Maybe.

The trust document should direct that the trustee has total discretion as to whether any income is to be distributed, with a further direction that the principal is not to be distributed. It can also stipulate that a trustee should *withhold income if the result would be the disqualification for government benefits.* Speak to your legal advisor about this, since some government agencies frown on using this method to qualify for benefits.

Money-Saving Suggestion

In the following example of a *testamentary trust,* it is the *later* estate of John (the beneficiary) that avoids estate tax:

I, JAMES SMITH, give and bequeath $100,000 to my trustee, XYZ Trust Company, IN TRUST NEVERTHELESS, and XYZ Trust Company is annually to distribute the income to my brother, JOHN

SMITH. Upon JOHN SMITH'S death, the XYZ Trust Company is to distribute the principal equally to the children of JOHN SMITH then surviving him.

(IN TRUST NEVERTHELESS means "in spite of that." So the possession of the money is given to the trust company but, in spite of that possession of the money, it is holding that money for the benefit of others, in this instance, John and his children.)

The estate of *James* does not save any money as a result of this testamentary trust. But upon the subsequent death of *John,* there is a double savings. First, the $100,000 does not pass through John's estate, so there is a *reduction in the executor's fee* because it is the trustee, not the executor, who distributes this trust principal upon John's death. Second, this $100,000 is *not included in John's taxable estate,* because he did not really own the $100,000; he had a limited use of the money (only the income derived from the principal).

One cost of having a testamentary trust is the fee paid annually to the trustee. Although this fee is an income tax deduction, I suggest you consider a testamentary trust only if there is a significant reason for its use. *The reason I find quite compelling is when the beneficiary of the trust would otherwise squander the inheritance if it were not supervised by a trustee.* But balance the benefits of using a trust with the possible economic frustration the beneficiary may feel because of the restricted availability of these funds. Emotional frustration is also experienced because the beneficiary feels inept, untrustworthy, and still *controlled by the deceased.*

YOUR ESTATE PLAN

All of us should think about our own death and the *disposition of our possessions after we are gone.* What is most important is our concern for those who survive us. If someone's survival has been dependent upon your economic assistance, you want that person to be able to continue without you. You also want those you leave behind to be able to spend their time in productive and enjoyable pursuits, not in long and involved attempts to complete the puzzle of your economic life.

In concluding Part One, let us review some of the major points discussed. An estate plan has been put together, and here is a summary:

You have gathered together all your important *legal documents.*

You have evaluated all your *insurance coverage.*

You have reviewed all your *investments,* and have created an *inventory of all your assets.*

You have chosen an *executor* to handle your estate.

You have chosen a *guardian* if you have a dependent child.

You have decided who are to be your *legatees.*

You have determined whether you want a *living will.*

You have located the deed to the *cemetery plot,* given directions for burial (and these directions might be included in your will), and you definitely have *discussed these directions with someone.*

You have signed your will and have told your executor where it is located.

Where do we go from here? Part Two will focus on *administering your estate,* which is the procedure for gathering and distributing your assets after you have died. In Part Three, the estate plan will be completed by reviewing the various *taxes* that must be paid by an estate. In Part Four, we will conclude our discussion by tying up loose ends regarding matters of life and death.

Sample Situation

Although the gathering together of your important documents might not be of great benefit to *you* (but it will make it easy for you to locate the information when you need it), in every case where the decedent had all the important documents in a safe place, the *executor's job* of administering the estate was always easier.

Money-Saving Suggestion

Here is a list of important documents and other vital information the originals of which should be kept in a safe place, perhaps in a safe deposit box, with photocopies at home:

your will

your tax returns for the past three years

your financial records for the past three years

the deed for your cemetery plot

the deed for your home

an inventory of your assets

your passport

life insurance policies

home insurance policy

bankbooks

Individual Retirement Accounts (IRAs)

certificates of deposit (CDs)

the name of the bank where your social security check is deposited

stock certificates

statements of employee benefits

statements of accrued sick leave

statements of accrued vacation

death certificates of close family members

your family tree

your birth certificate

military discharge papers

divorce decree(s)

your completed living will

trust agreements

the location of your safe deposit box

proof of any debt owed to you (IOUs, contracts, letters of agreement, liens, etc.)

proof of any debt you owe (invoices, contracts, IOUs, letters of agreement, etc.)

a list of credit card accounts

the names and addresses of your doctor, lawyer, and accountant.

I include military discharge papers on my list because your executor might refer to them if your burial is to be in a national cemetery, or if your survivors want to receive a flag in tribute to your military sacrifice.

Why do I advise you to retain copies of the death certificates of close family members? As you will learn in Part Two, some states require your executor to contact your next of kin at the time of your death in order to give them an opportunity to question the legality of your will. Therefore, by having copies of death certificates for departed close family members, it will be an easier job for your executor to show the court how the identity of your surviving next of kin was determined.

If you cannot find any of the information on this list, locate it (or replace it) immediately. Keep in mind that almost everyone knows where most of this information can be found. But it is those few missing items that will cause problems. *Find (or replace) them now!*

Let us now see what happens in the administration of a deceased person's estate.

Part Two

After Death

9

Introduction

PROVING THE WILL (PROBATE)

A general understanding of the probate process is necessary because this is the first legal activity in the administration of an estate. Here is an overview, which will be expanded upon in chapter 11.

The probate process, undertaken by the person named in the will as executor, consists of (1) filing the will and the affidavit of the witnesses in court; (2) producing the death certificate; (3) notifying the legatees and all those who would inherit (the next of kin) if the will were successfully challenged; and (4) *concluding with the court's decision that this document is the deceased's will* or, alternatively, that the document is not a legal will. Through probate—and the court's approval of the will—the named executor is authorized to begin to administer the estate. The executor's seal of approval, issued by the court, is a legal document known in most states as *letters testamentary*.

Probate can be delayed by either of two occurrences: the will is *challenged* by the next of kin, or the executor *cannot locate* the next of kin. In either of these sources of probate delay the court can grant a preliminary authorization that allows the named executor to act on the testator's behalf. Permission is granted to the executor named in a will, which has not yet been approved by the court, to safeguard the estate's assets. This preliminary authorization, however, does not allow the executor to distribute any assets to the legatees. This preliminary authorization is aptly referred to as *preliminary letters testamentary*.

Keep in mind the distinction between probate assets and gross assets of the deceased. *Probate assets* include only those *assets distributed by the will. Gross assets* are the *total assets* owned by the deceased. Therefore, gross assets include not only the probate assets but also many nonprobate assets (assets that pass by right of survivorship) such as: joint bank accounts, insurance policies with a named beneficiary, jointly owned real estate, and "in trust for" (or "payment on death") accounts. Later in this chapter we will take a look at joint bank accounts and "in trust for" bank accounts.

Sample Situation

During probate, problems sometimes arise between the person named as the executor and the attorney he or she has chosen. Predictably, these problems are about money, namely *the attorney's fee.*

The question of fees should be resolved at the first meeting between the executor designate and the attorney who is being interviewed. This meeting should take place shortly after the testator's death. The decision on the fee should be confirmed in writing, and both people should sign it. The designated executor should remember to sign the agreement, not as an individual, but on behalf of the estate. Then, shortly after being appointed as the executor, this employment contract can be reaffirmed.

The amount of the attorney's fee varies from state to state. But even individual attorneys within the same community have different fees. The fee, however, is generally about two to four percent of the value of the estate.

Money-Saving Suggestion

At the meeting scheduled by the person named in the will (but not yet appointed by the court) as executor, perhaps a next of kin or a major legatee should also attend. He or she might be a good source of information.

At this meeting try to spend a couple of hours in presenting information to the attorney such as: income tax returns, the names and addresses of next of kin, whether any assets require special safeguarding, and a general review of the deceased's asset inventory. *Discuss possible problems,* such as the survivors' immediate need for cash. If the estate gets off to a good start, there is usually clear sailing ahead. The opposite, unfortunately, is also true.

Avoid the pitfall of trying to do too much at this first meeting. Your goal should be to identify and discuss possible problems, rather than attempting to resolve them. The initial meeting should last no longer than two hours. *If it is well organized by the attorney, a lot of information can be communicated.* Survivors are tense and upset after a loved one's death, and a two-hour meeting is long enough. Also, remember that the attorney is only being interviewed; there is no need for you to hire this particular lawyer.

ADMINISTERING AN ESTATE

After the will is probated, the property of the deceased is gathered; any debts owed by the deceased are paid; and the remaining assets are then distributed to the legatees. This process—gathering and distributing the assets of the deceased—is called *administering an estate,* which can be accomplished in as little as a few months, or it could take years.

When administering the estate, it is important to know who is in charge. If there is a will, then the *executor* is in charge of gathering and distributing the deceased's assets. If there is no will, then the court appoints an administrator (usually the closest relative of the deceased or the closest relatives of the deceased if they are of equal degree of kinship) who is responsible for performing these tasks. No one can force you to become the administrator; but, as next of kin, you have the legal right to ask the court to appoint you as the administrator. The executor or the administrator (if there is no will) is referred to as *the personal representative of the estate.* As you know, the executor's identification is *letters testamentary;* the administrator's identification is *letters of administration.*

Which debts must the estate pay? Only those debts that the deceased would have had to pay, along with those necessary debts incurred by the estate, are paid by the personal representative out of the deceased's assets.

So who gets what's left? An asset of the deceased is distributed in one of four ways: (1) If the deceased had a will, assets owned go to the legatees named in the will. (2) If the deceased did not have a will, assets owned go to the next of kin. (3) If the deceased owned an asset jointly with someone and there is the right of the survivor to own the entire asset (for example, if John and Mary owned a bank account jointly with a right of survivorship), then the surviving owner receives the asset. (4) If an asset was owned by the deceased but was in trust for someone (for example, John had a bank account in trust for Mary), then the person it is in trust for receives the asset. We will learn more about *joint ownership* and *in trust for ownership* later in this chapter. But for now let me stress one idea on joint ownership: I recommend that the document setting out such joint ownership state that there is *a right of survivorship,* thus making your intention absolutely clear to everyone that, when one owner dies, the survivor will own the entire asset. If you do not want the other person on the account to own it when you die, then use neither joint ownership nor name a beneficiary on an "in trust for" account. Unfortunately, sometimes there is confusion as to the legal effect of a joint account. A person might put a trusted person's name on an account just for the convenience of having that person available to make a withdrawal, *not knowing that upon death the other person has a claim to the entire account.*

Sample Situation

How long does it take to administer an estate? A recent report from the Office of the Attorney General of New York State gives case histories of estates that have continued for more than a quarter century. But don't despair. Most estates are administered within a year or two, and there is no need for this to be a traumatic experience.

Some states have a requirement that legacies be paid within a short time after death. However, even if the state of domicile of the deceased does not have this requirement, the executor should try to distribute the assets within a year after death. There is the procedure whereby a partial distribution of the legacy can be made, and a portion can be retained for contingencies such as debts and taxes. Those who have been waiting for more than a year for an executor to make a distribution to them from an estate should get on the telephone right away and arrange to meet with the executor and with the attorney for the estate. *Find out the cause of the delay.*

Money-Saving Suggestions

Your state might have an expedited procedure for small estates. It involves less paperwork, is less costly, and is quicker. You do not need an attorney. Find out the dollar amount in your state's definition of a small estate. It can be anywhere from a couple of thousand dollars up to almost one hundred thousand dollars.

Keep in mind that the amount refers to those assets owned solely by the deceased and without a named beneficiary. An estate with hundreds of thousands of dollars in assets, such as joint accounts, but only a few thousand dollars of assets in the sole name of the deceased, is eligible for the small estate procedure. Use of this expedited procedure, if applicable, should be considered by the executor. If this route is chosen, the need to hire an attorney might be eliminated. However, often it is difficult to determine clearly whether legal service is required, and the only solution is this ironic fact: you must see an attorney to find out if an attorney is needed. Books, newspaper articles, and lectures will not give you the answer. Remember, the legal cost of preventing a problem is usually less than the legal cost of correcting a problem.

Here is a suggestion to a legatee. Ask the executor for the approximate date when you will receive your legacy; request to be notified of any delays that result in an adjusted timetable. You are politely letting the executor know that you *will not tolerate any unnecessary delays.*

JOINT ACCOUNT

A joint account has two or more owners. When one owner dies, then the other owner(s) assume(s) possession of the deceased's share of the joint account. There are two important points to remember about joint accounts:

First, since the surviving person on the account becomes sole owner of the account when the other joint owner dies, the funds in this account do not go through the probate proceeding. *This lowers the cost of probate.*

Second, *estate tax is NOT lessened by having someone else's name on the account.* If John has a $100,000 certificate of deposit and puts his niece's name on the account, this $100,000 *is included* in John's taxable estate. We will now learn why this is so.

The IRS presumes that the asset was owned *entirely by the first to die.* (The exception to this rule is an asset jointly owned by spouses, where the conclusion is that one-half is owned by each of them. More about this exception, and how it might affect you, in Part Four.)

Therefore, suppose a rich uncle adds a poor young niece's name to his bank account. Upon his death the presumption is that he owned it (and it is included in his taxable estate). What is particularly troublesome, however, is that if the *niece dies first,* there is the presumption that the niece owned it (and it is included in *her* taxable estate). The personal representative of the niece's estate would then have the burden of disproving the presumption that *the entire amount in the account belonged* to her.

Another problem that results from putting someone else's name on the account is that you lose the tax-saving opportunity of having this money fund a testamentary trust. This is because the surviving person named on the account owns the entire account at the moment of the other joint owner's death (unless this surviving person disclaimed ownership). Therefore, the money in the account is not available to fund the testamentary trust.

For those of you who have joint accounts, this right of survivorship should be clearly stated on the account *in order to assure that the surviving owner receives the entire account.* Again, I advise that this *right of survivorship* be stated in all situations (assuming this is what you want), whether or not your bank or your state law requires it. Once again, if this is not what is intended, then do not enter into a joint account.

Sample Situations

Let us look at some joint account questions and answers in the case of wealthy John and his invalid niece, Mary.

There is a joint bank account with a right of survivorship in the names of John and Mary. *Upon John's death who receives the money in the account?* Mary receives it, even if John's will says otherwise. This saves probate costs.

John's net worth is $700,000, and Mary has no assets. John decides to put Mary's name on all of his accounts. *Does this affect John's taxable estate by reducing its value?* No. The $700,000 is included in John's estate.

Suppose John wants his sickly niece, Mary, to be financially secure. *Should the niece's name be put on John's accounts?* Probably not, although if the niece's name is on the accounts, the niece does receive the money. But if she is sick, who will look after the money? I would advise John to consider either establishing a *living trust* or having a *testamentary trust* as part of his will. By following either of these suggestions, John assures that there is someone to look after the money on the niece's behalf.

But what if John lists Mary's name on all his bankbooks as a joint owner. *Has he made a gift to Mary?* Does she withdraw money from the account? Does he intend now to give her a half-interest in the account, or is he putting her name on the account only to avoid probate? See your attorney before putting names on accounts, because if a gift of over $10,000 is made, a federal gift tax return must be filed. Once again, you will learn about taxes, including gift taxes, in Part Three.

John lists Mary's name on all of his bankbooks. *Can Mary's creditors look to these assets for payment of Mary's bills?* Yes. This is a serious problem with joint ownership, because jointly owned property can be attached by creditors of either owner.

Money-Saving Suggestions

For smaller estates, a joint account is advisable. This is because the money passes to the other person owning the account, without going through the probate process (which costs money, including the executor's fee and the attorney's fee).

For larger estates, the concern should be about estate taxes, and to reduce these taxes you might decide to use a testamentary trust. If so, you should not have all your money in joint accounts. This is because joint accounts go directly to the other person and *thus there is no money available to fund a testamentary trust.*

THE "IN TRUST FOR" ACCOUNT

The individual who owns such an account *names the person who is to receive the account when the owner dies.* An example of this would be a bank account under the title of *Mary in trust for Ann.* This is called a totten trust account. Another example is a savings bond owned by *Mary in trust for Ann.* Usually the words "in trust for" are abbreviated to *i.t.f.* Here are three important facts to know about an "in trust for" account (also known as "payment on death" account):

Who receives the money in the account upon the owner's death? *The money is received by the person named on the account.*

What are the estate tax consequences? There is no estate tax savings, because *the money is included in the account owner's estate.*

Do not confuse the "in trust for" account with a living trust or a testamentary trust. The "in trust for" account has no trustee controlling the money; it is just a way of transferring the money, without probate, to the named beneficiary on the account.

"In trust for" accounts share three similarities with joint accounts: both reduce probate costs, neither saves any estate tax dollars, and both prevent the dollars in these accounts from being used to fund a testamentary trust.

How do a joint account and an "in trust for" account differ? The joint account may be owned by all individuals named on the account, or it may be owned by only one individual on the account. This can be confusing. However, the "in trust for" account is owned only by the first name on the account; *the person it is held in trust for has no ownership of the account until the owner dies.*

If asked to choose between a joint account and an "in trust for" account, I prefer the latter. Not everyone can be trusted, so I do not like the idea of someone else's name appearing as joint owner on a financial asset. The "in trust for" account avoids the question raised in the previous section, on joint accounts, as to whether there is a taxable gift to someone named as a joint owner of your property. Furthermore, unlike the joint account, *the "in trust for" account cannot be a source of payment of the beneficiary's creditors,* and the beneficiary has no control over the asset.

Sample Situation

James has a net worth of $150,000, which is invested in a bank account. He desires that upon his death his son, John, is to receive this money. Should the account be in the form of an "in trust for" account with John as the named beneficiary? Possibly. However, James may decide that it is better to leave John a $150,000 legacy in a testamentary trust, so that John does not squander the legacy. Here is what James might say in his will:

> I give and bequeath $150,000, to my trustee, ABC Trust Company, in trust, and it is to distribute the income annually to my son, John, and upon the death of John, my trustee is to distribute the $150,000 evenly among John's children.

In addition to assuring that son John has income for every year of his life, this testamentary trust also assures that the grandchildren eventually receive this money. If James has the money in an "in trust for" account or in a joint account with John, it goes automatically to John, and therefore is not *available to fund the testamentary trust.*

Money-Saving Suggestion

You have been advised to be cautious in your use of a joint account. This advice also applies to your use of an "in trust for" account. For a wealthy individual, the reduced probate costs are small when compared to the benefits of using a testamentary trust. In the above sample situation, James possibly concluded that it is better not to have his estate avoid the probate costs because he wanted the legacy to John to be *controlled* by a trustee.

Now that these preliminary introductory matters have been put behind us, we can begin our discussion of administering an estate.

10

Preliminary Activities

OBITUARY; SECURING THE HOME

Is it a good idea to publish the obituary of a loved one? It is a personal decision that has to be made by the person closest to the deceased, probably by the person who will be the executor. But here are four reasons for doing so. The main reason is to *advise people of the death*. However, close friends and relatives should be telephoned, because many people do not read the obituary page of the newspaper. The second reason is to *honor the deceased*. Surely, however, it is better to have said nice things directly to the person rather than wait until after the person is dead; only the survivors hear the kind words extolling the virtues of the deceased's life. The third reason is that *a charity can be suggested as the recipient of contributions*. The fourth reason is that it may be a good research source for an executor in some future estate *seeking the identity of a deceased's next of kin* (the subject of the next money-saving suggestion). Share your own thoughts on the subject of an obituary with your executor.

Be aware that an obituary advises criminals in our society that a home may be standing vacant, particularly at the time of burial. Valuable possessions (jewelry and the like) should not be kept in the deceased's empty home. Safeguard the home; for security reasons some families arrange for a house sitter during the funeral.

In addition to potential burglary, some families have expressed other reasons for not publishing an obituary. Unscrupulous people sometimes use an obituary column as a referral source for business. Estates have been preyed upon by real estate brokers, appraisers, attorneys, investment advisors, charities, merchants, stock brokers, creditors, and others. Be *cautious* in dealing with every provider of service who solicits your business after the death of a loved one. Better yet, have *no dealings* with these people. If you are contacted by someone you do not know, most likely your name was obtained from the obituary. Try not to make any major decisions at this time; but if you do, consult only *trusted friends and advisors.*

Sample Situation

It is a sad fact that many homes are burglarized during a funeral service. The criminal reads the obituary and notes the time of burial. In the case of the deceased who lived alone, this threat continues for as long as property remains in the deceased's last residence. Many people are aware that there is now a permanently vacant home.

As I tell my clients, be careful! *Make sure the home is secured.*

Money-Saving Suggestion

As you know, when a person dies, the next of kin are sought for one of two reasons: either the deceased did have a will, and they are the people who might possibly contest it; or the deceased did not have a will, and they are the people who are entitled to inherit the deceased's property.

Obituaries are a good vehicle for *locating the next of kin.* Suppose the deceased had *no immediate family.* Further suppose that both the mother and father of the deceased had numerous brothers and sisters, but the identities of most of them are unknown. All these maternal and paternal aunts and uncles are the deceased's next of kin. If the dates of death for some of these relatives are known, I suggest that the personal representative of the estate *research the local newspapers in the communities where these deceased persons last resided.* New family information can be discovered through obituaries of other family members. (An outstanding source for locating obituaries is the Genealogical Society of the Church of Jesus Christ of Latter-Day Saints. Its catalogues contain literally millions of obituaries.)

FUNERAL EXPENSES

Part of the job of administering an estate is arranging for the disposal of the body. Cremation is an alternative to a more costly funeral. Throughout history, some organized religious groups have opposed cremation, but these barriers have essentially disappeared. If cremation was not the deceased's preference (and the executor should know this), I give you the following list of goods and services provided by a funeral home:

Minimum Services:

Personnel available twenty-four hours a day.

Coordinating plans with the cemetery.

Completion of the required forms to obtain the death certificate and the permit for the disposition of the body.

Additional Services:

Coordination of the funeral ceremony.

Preparation of Remains:

Embalming

Cosmetic preparation

Facilities:

Use of facilities for viewing.

Other Goods:

Acknowledgment cards

Prayer cards

Casket:

In addition to the casket there might be an outer burial container.

Other Charges:

Transportation

Cemetery fee

Pallbearers

Musicians

Gratuities

Obituary notice

Certified copies of the death certificate

Sample Situation

You—not your surviving spouse, executor, relative, or friend—must decide about the funeral. It is appropriate for everyone—not just for the person who is seriously ill—to tell the executor, spouse, friend, or close relative what funeral arrangements are desired. I know this is a difficult topic, but having this discussion makes the survivor's job somewhat easier.

Money-Saving Suggestion

If you are the person entrusted with the funeral arrangements, be sure you know what it is that you are purchasing and what alternative choices are available. Be a smart shopper, even in time of tragedy.

You have learned that probate means "proving the will." Let us look at the procedure this "proving" entails.

11

Probate Procedure

LOCATING THE WILL

The person has died, the obituary has been published, and the burial has taken place. What next?

Is there a will? If the deceased was careful about preparing and planning the estate, someone would have been told the location of the will (and also the location of all the other important papers). But if it is not known whether the deceased had a will (or if it is known that a will does exist, but no one is sure where it is), here are some suggestions on how best to go about searching for the will:

Ask *relatives* of the deceased if they have any knowledge of a will. While difficult to do during the time of burial, this is nevertheless the best opportunity you'll have, because the clan is all gathered together.

Search the *house* of the deceased. Do not discard anything.

Find out if the deceased had a *safe deposit box*. One way to do this is to review the *cancelled checks* of the previous year in search of the annual payment for the safe deposit box rent. Since the safe deposit box rental payment is a miscellaneous itemized deduction, look at the previous year's tax return and accompanying records to find out whether the deceased rented one.

Find out if the deceased had an *attorney*. Look again through the cancelled checks to see if an attorney's fee was paid.

Check the *courthouse;* perhaps the will is on file. In most states a will can be placed in the safekeeping of the court during the testator's lifetime.

Visit the local *banks;* perhaps a bank is named as executor and is holding the will.

An easy way to go about searching for the will is to go *where the testator told you the will is kept.*

Another easy way is to look at the *testator's inventory,* which should identify the location of the will. You, as testator, can make it easy for your executor to locate your will.

It is a crime to hide or destroy the will of a deceased person. Obviously this is a difficult law to enforce, and violations often go undetected. Therefore, when making a will, *give serious consideration to having your executor retain possession of the document—or at least a copy.* (An exception to this would be an executor who is receiving *less through your will* than the person would receive *if you died without a will.* Do not offer this temptation to your executor: *the temptation to destroy the will.*) Also, your *attorney's vault* is a possible depository for your will.

Sample Situation

Most states have laws that provide a procedure whereby a person who possibly has possession of a deceased's will can be forced to appear in court. This person is then required to give sworn testimony as to whether he or she has the will or knows its whereabouts. If this testimony reveals the existence of a will, then it must be produced for probate.

Many times the situation of the recalcitrant person who has the will is quickly resolved by this court proceeding. Often the person just keeps putting off bringing the will to the court's attention, *without intending to conceal the document.* Sadly, however, I am sure there are cases where a person dies, someone has the deceased's will, and the document is never produced. If no one else knows that there is a will, then the deceased's estate is administered as if the person had died intestate.

Money-Saving Suggestions

Do not sign duplicate copies of your will. All signed copies must be produced in court. (Keep in mind that a photocopy is not a signed copy; there is nothing wrong in having photocopies of your original will, but be sure the person doing the photocopying *does not remove the staples.*) If a *signed copy* that was in the testator's possession cannot be produced, *the law presumes that the testator revoked the will by destroying it.* Therefore, *by not signing duplicate copies,* you save the executor the trouble of searching for all the signed duplicates. Furthermore, you will have avoided the calamity of your last will and testament being denied probate because of the mistaken belief that you had revoked any one of these signed duplicates by destroying it.

As you already know, you are always free to have a *new will* prepared. If you do, the old will is automatically revoked in favor of the new will, whose later date makes *it* the document to be probated. (What I do not recommend is *multiple signed originals of the same will;* one is enough. If someone knows that you had in your possession *multiple* signed originals of the same will, your executor will be *required to produce all of them.*)

I also suggest that when you ask the person close to you to be your executor, tell that person where you keep all your important papers, including your will.

DETERMINING THE DOMICILE

As you know, the person named in a will as executor petitions the court to obtain letters testamentary. This process of probating the will is undertaken in the *state where the deceased was domiciled.*

The word *domicile* is derived from the Latin word for home. *Domicile is the place where a person has a permanent home.* A person acquires a domicile by living there and having no definite present intention of later moving from there. Domicile entails not only residence in fact but also intent to make that residence one's home. Do not be confused by these definitions of domicile, because, for most of you, your domicile is *where you live.* The problem arises either when you are in the middle of a move or when you have two or more houses.

In which state are *you* domiciled? If you are not sure of the answer (perhaps you have homes in Michigan and Florida), you can be sure that the various states where you now live will someday be fighting over the question of your domicile. The answer has *estate tax consequences,* in that either or both states might attempt to impose an estate tax. The answer to the domicile question also determines which state law controls these issues: e.g., what are the *requirements for a valid will,* who are your next of kin, what protection from disinheritance is given to a spouse, what rights are given to creditors of the estate, and so on. The first issue—*requirements for a valid will*—is a most important one. If your domicile changes to another state, then your will should be *reviewed by an attorney in your new state to assure that it meets the new state's requirements.*

I am not suggesting anything so drastic as selling your vacation home in order to eliminate any question about your domicile. But you should decide which home is your *permanent* home, then be consistent. The following should be concentrated in your state of domicile: voter registration, driver's license, automobile registration, recorded place of residence for federal tax return purposes, residence as indicated on employer records, the address at which you receive your pension check(s) and social security checks, and the location where you serve on jury duty.

The problem arises when two or more states have a claim that you *permanently reside within their borders.* Take the example of a retired automotive employee who votes in Florida and lists a Florida address on his federal tax return; but perhaps this same person registers his automobile and obtains his driver's license in Michigan, has General Motors pension checks and social security checks sent to his Michigan address, and is on the Michigan jury roster. At the time of death, both states will feel compelled to claim the person as a resident, since each state has what it believes to be firm grounds for doing so. You can avoid this problem if you decide which is your state, that is, where you have your permanent home. After your choice has been made, be consistent in listing this state on all vital records.

Sample Situation

Even where questions of domicile do not arise, two states may be involved in the administration of an estate. This occurs when a deceased owned real property (land, a home, or other building) in a state other than the domiciliary state, because *after an owner's death, the transfer of any real property is affected by the law of the state where it is located.* Take, for example, the situation of a person who had a permanent home in Michigan, but owned a winter home in another state. The will is probated in Michigan, the state where the deceased was domiciled. The other state then requires what is called an *ancillary probate proceeding.* Normally the state where real property is owned accepts *the will admitted to probate in the domiciliary state,* and issues ancillary letters testamentary to the executor. Ownership of the real property then is transferred to the person named in the will. The transfer of personal property—anything other than real property—(such as your bankbook, bonds, jewelry, etc.) is controlled by the state where you were domiciled. This is true even if you own bonds issued by, have a bank account in, or possess any other property (other than real property) connected to another state.

Money-Saving Suggestions

In almost all cases where there is a question of the deceased's domicile, the issue arises because the *deceased* never decided which state would be the home state. *State your domicile at the beginning of the will.* This is done simply by listing your address. While this does not prevent the problem of two state jurisdictions doing battle over tax dollars, my suggestion will cause *you* to analyze *the question of domicile* and clearly decide which state is the domiciliary state. Then be *consistent.*

To those of you who plan to buy real property in a state other than your domiciliary state, consider having a *joint owner (with the right of survivorship)* on the deed. This avoids an ancillary probate proceeding in the nondomiciliary state, although it does not avoid the payment of that state's estate tax based on the value of the land, the house, or other building owned there.

LOCATING THE NEXT OF KIN

In some jurisdictions, the person named in the will as executor has to prove to the court that *all the next of kin have been notified* and that none of them are contesting the will. The proof is a statement, signed by the next of kin and submitted to the court, waiving the rights of these persons to contest the will. A next of kin who does not waive this right is advised by the court of the date when a challenge to the will must commence. In other jurisdictions *the will is just filed in court,* and the court waits a short period of time to see if anyone comes forward to challenge the document. These other jurisdictions are, obviously, less protective of the rights of the next of kin.

Notification of the next of kin, those who would receive the deceased's probate assets if the will is denied probate, prevents bogus wills from being probated. Who else is better motivated to assure the legality of the will than those who would most benefit from the court's rejection of the document? Do not get confused about this notification process. This confusion can best be illustrated by a brother who had survived his two sisters: one sister died *with* a will, and the court notified him; another sister died *without* a will, and the court also notified him. That's right. In the first case he was notified that, as next of kin, he has a right to *challenge the sister's will;* in the second case he was notified that, as next of kin, he is to *receive the sister's estate assets.*

Locating the next of kin is quite simple in most situations. However, it can be complicated when the deceased *is not survived by any close relatives.* Many families have not been in this country for more than two generations, so the search for the next of kin often takes the executor to some far-off lands. The typical search procedure for the next of kin of one who is *not survived by any close relatives* is to trace the brothers and sisters of both parents of the deceased, and if all these aunts and uncles are deceased, then look for the children and grandchildren of these aunts and uncles. As you know, the children of your aunts and uncles are your first cousins. Perhaps you do not know that the *children of your first cousins are called your first cousins once removed* and, furthermore, you might not know of their existence.

Let me restate this while you think of your own family tree, but with some adjustments. *Assume you do not have an immediate family, and you never met any of your aunts or uncles.* Their children are your first cousins, and your first cousins' children are your first cousins once removed. So, if you have no close family members, and your aunts and uncles stayed in a foreign country, it could be difficult to locate all your next of kin, because you may be looking for your first cousins once removed. However, in most situations a person's next of kin are quite easy to determine, and you might want to refer to the first chapter of this book to refresh your memory about the guidelines for who is your next of kin.

Sample Situation

One case that comes to mind is that of an elderly woman whose husband had predeceased her. The woman had no children and no brothers or sisters; both of her parents had come from Europe, and they had *numerous brothers and sisters, all of whom were deceased.* They had a number of children (her first cousins). It was difficult to locate all these children; however, it was necessary because they were the next of kin.

What is interesting about this case is that both sides of the elderly woman's family tree *(her mother's side and her father's side)* were missing, making it doubly difficult to locate the next of kin. Notice, when I refer to both sides of a person's family tree, I refer to the person's *parents*. Do not confuse this with in-laws; *your spouse's family are not your next of kin.* But relatives, both on your mother's side of your family and on your father's side of your family, may be your next of kin (as in the above situation). If you do not have parents, spouse, children, brothers or sisters, nieces or nephews, aunts or uncles, then your next of kin are your first cousins. Your first cousins on your father's side of the family are the same relationship to you as your first cousins on your mother's side of the family. In some families, identifying all these first cousins can take some time. There are companies that specialize in locating relatives. These genealogical searches can be expensive; therefore, I recommend that you carefully check the credentials of the company you hire, and consult with your attorney before you engage its services.

Money-Saving Suggestions

If out-of-town legatees and distributees visit for the funeral, the executor should obtain their names and addresses so as to have this information when it comes time to notify them that a will is offered for probate. They are also good sources of information in locating any other relatives who may be the legatees or next of kin of the deceased.

Again, keep in mind that instances of no close next of kin *do not occur too frequently.* Even when the situation does occur and the next of kin are as remote as first cousins once removed, *often the identity of these individuals is known.* If this is your situation, here is my suggestion: give their names and addresses to your executor. It is unfortunate indeed when a person *knows that his or her next of kin are distant relatives, knows their identity and location, but takes this information to the grave.*

CHALLENGES TO A WILL

If your will has been prepared carefully by you and your attorney, then the chance of anyone contesting it is remote. Your next of kin, nevertheless, may still challenge the will. A legatee named in an earlier will also has the right to contest a later will (or codicil) if the legacy to be received was more under the earlier document. This is fair. How else can society assure that bogus wills are not being presented for probate? Our laws, therefore, allow a challenge by those who would receive the assets of the deceased if the will is not valid.

If someone does choose to challenge the will, there are a few possible resolutions to this problem. The challenger (known as the *contestant*) and the executor may seek to *settle* the will dispute, wherein the contesting next of kin receives something in return for withdrawing the claim that the will is not valid. This would occur in a situation where the deceased's testamentary capacity was marginal, and the legatees and the next of kin—the adversaries in the proceeding—decide to *compromise*. Alternatively, the probate judge may *dismiss* the contestant's challenge because it has no merit. The final possibility is to have all questions presented and argued in a *trial*. Incidentally, if there is a trial, the right to a jury depends on the law of the domiciliary state of the deceased. The U.S. Constitution does not guarantee a jury trial to those contesting a will; however, some states have a statutory provision allowing for such jury trials.

Here are two suggestions that might help avoid challenges to a will. *Do not tell* your potential legatees that they are to receive something from your estate. If you do and then later change your mind and execute a new will, those people given an unfulfilled promise of a legacy may express their disappointment by challenging the will.

My second suggestion is that you *clearly express your intentions in your will.* Remember my earlier suggestion that if you leave your automobile to a particular legatee, the will should identify the automobile as the one you own at the time of your death. Do not leave a legatee your 1991 Chevrolet. When you die you may own the year 2021 model. If the "almost owner" of the automobile is also a next of kin, then this type of ambiguity may be enough to enrage the person, who then challenges the will.

There are relatively few challenges to a will. It may appear, however, that there are many will contests due to the publicity given to the occasional one. As for the outcome of such challenges, most are settled before going to trial.

Sample Situation

The most expensive probate occurs when some one or more persons contest the will. Probably the longest and most expensive challenge in history was over the will of Matthias, the Hapsburg Emperor. Bohemia rejected the heir, Ferdinand II, named in Matthias's will. The challenge resulted in the Thirty Years War.

The following situation is the most bizarre will contest that has come to my attention. The next of kin of the deceased were his three siblings: a disinherited brother who challenged the will and two sisters who were bequeathed the entire estate. The two sisters, aware that their deceased brother probably lacked testamentary capacity, *graciously decided to divide the small estate equally among all three surviving siblings.* Although a total victory for the brother who had been disinherited, *he was not happy with this generous settlement.* From this situation I learned that there is a thrill to attacking a will and that such thrill can be as pleasurable as gaining a financial reward.

Money-Saving Suggestions

In many cases where a will is contested, the argument raised by the next of kin is that the deceased lacked the testamentary capacity necessary to execute the document. Here it is imperative that the *executor act quickly to obtain statements from those who knew the deceased.* Doctors, household help, friends, and relatives are good sources of statements. The reason I suggest that the executor act quickly is because *you want to be the first person obtaining the statements of those who knew the deceased.* I have found that people sometimes answer questions based on how a question is asked. I am not suggesting that such people are lying, but pollsters know that *people express satisfaction when asked to tell some good things about someone,* and they express dissatisfaction when asked to tell some bad things about someone.

Do not allow the fear of a challenge by a next of kin to prevent you from having a will prepared. To permit this fear to prevent you from having a will drawn *allows your next of kin to receive your estate.*

RENUNCIATION BY THE EXECUTOR

If you are named the executor in a will, the first decision you have to make is whether or not you want to serve in this capacity.

Some reasons for *not wanting to serve* (and thus *renouncing* appointment as executor) are that you do not have the *time,* the *energy,* the *talent,* or the *patience* required to administer an estate; perhaps it is too *depressing* a job; possibly you *dislike* the next of kin or those named as legatees in the will. Whatever your reason, *you can renounce.* However, *it is better to say no when asked by the testator,* rather than exercising your right to renounce sometime later after the testator's death. Keep in mind that if you decide to renounce your appointment as executor, *you still have the obligation to bring the will to the court's attention.*

One reason you might *want to serve as executor* is because you *loved* the deceased and want to see the person's life's work brought to a smooth conclusion. Another reason is because you receive a *fee* for this service. Your fee, although varying from state to state, is approximately three to four percent of the value of the assets you administer. A third reason to serve is because you may be receiving a significant *legacy,* and you want to see that things are done right.

While you are serving as executor, you might decide to *resign* before you complete the job of administering the estate. Upon resigning, you must usually account to the court for the estate assets you have gathered and distributed. Another situation that can occur is the *death* of an executor before the end of the administration of the estate. In this instance, the *deceased executor's executor* files an account with the court, and a successor is appointed.

Assume you have neither initially renounced your appointment nor resigned or died during your service as executor. There is still another possibility. While you are serving as executor, a person interested in the estate can petition the court for your *removal.* Reasons for this move might be alleged negligence, conflict of interest, or lack of activity in the administration of the estate.

If the executor named in the will *renounces, resigns, dies while serving, or is removed, who becomes the new executor and, therefore, the new holder of letters testamentary?* A carefully drawn will provides for this contingency. Do you remember my suggestion that your will should name a person or bank as the *successor executor?* If the primary executor fails to become the executor (or after assuming the role ceases to function due to death, resignation, or removal), *this successor executor becomes the new executor and receives letters testamentary.* If a successor executor is not named in the will, then the court appoints someone to administer the estate. The next of kin or one of the legatees named in the will is the likely person to be appointed.

Sample Situations

There are two cases in which an executor is advised to waive the fee for performing this function. In cases where a surviving spouse serves as executor, if the executor's fee is not waived, it is subject to income tax. To illustrate, let us assume that a wife's net estate is worth $100,000, and she leaves all of it to her husband, who is designated the executor. Let us further assume that the state law provides for an executor's fee in the amount of three percent of the probate estate. Thus the husband receives a $97,000 legacy free of federal estate tax, because *what a spouse receives is free of any federal estate tax as a result of the estate tax marital deduction.* The husband also receives a $3,000 executor's fee, which is subject to federal income tax. But by waiving the executor's fee, the husband receives $100,000 completely free of any federal *estate* or *income* tax.

The second situation is similar but with a different family relationship. Assume a widow has a net estate of $100,000, and she leaves it all to her son, who has been designated the executor. As in the above case, let us assume that the state law provides for an executor's fee in the amount of three percent of the probate estate. Thus the son receives a $97,000 legacy free of federal estate tax, *because there is no federal estate tax on estates up to $600,000 (in addition to any amount a spouse receives).* The son also receives a $3,000 executor's fee, which is subject to federal income tax. But again, by waiving the executor's fee, the son receives $100,000 free of any federal *estate* or *income* tax.

Keep in mind, however, that if an estate *is* subject to an estate tax (for example, if it exceeds $600,000), there might be a tax savings by *accepting this commission.* Consider the following: John is the *executor and sole legatee* of an estate with substantial assets. If John's individual income tax on this commission is 28 percent of the commission *received by him,* and the estate tax savings is 40 percent of this expense *paid by it,* then John *should receive* the commission. Why? Because the tax *legally avoided* by the estate *exceeds the income tax owed by John.*

Money-Saving Suggestion

You may decide at the time you are having your will prepared that it is tax-wise to have your executor serve without a fee, and you can state so in your will. Here is a will clause that implements this suggestion:

> I expressly direct that my executor (or my successor executor, if serving) is not to receive any fee or commission.

This clause eliminates the need for the executor to waive the fee.

The obituary has been published, the funeral has been conducted, the will has been located and presented to the court in the jurisdiction where the deceased was domiciled, the next of kin have been contacted, the will has not been contested, and the executor has accepted his or her appointment. How does an executor prove this status?

12

Results of Probate

IDENTIFICATION OF THE PERSONAL REPRESENTATIVE

Probate results in the issuance of a document to the executor. In many states this document is called *letters testamentary*. You already know about this document; it was introduced in Part One, in our discussion of whom to choose as executor; it was again explained during our discussion of probate. As you also already know, if a person dies *without a will,* the relative appointed by the court to administer the estate (*the administrator*) receives a document similar to letters testamentary. In many states this document is aptly called *letters of administration.* Whether an executor or administrator, this person is called the *personal representative of the estate.*

A copy of the letters testamentary or the letters of administration must be produced to those individuals transacting business with the personal representative of the estate. For example, a bank holding money in the name of the deceased never releases this money to the personal representative of the estate without first receiving a copy of either the letters testamentary or the letters of administration. Also, if real estate owned by the deceased is to be sold, a buyer of the real estate never accepts a deed signed by the personal representative of the estate without first receiving a copy of the letters testamentary or the letters of administration. Such letters attest that the executor or administrator is empowered to act on behalf of the estate.

After the court has issued letters testamentary or letters of administration, the actions of the executor or administrator are supervised by the court. This supervision has come under criticism in recent years for being unnecessarily *complicated* and *expensive*. Since many estates are resolved in a friendly fashion, this supervision *often is unnecessary*. In my opinion, however, it serves a good purpose, even though it is not needed for every estate. Even if court supervision is proven to be *unnecessary* in nine out of every ten estates, it would be an impossible job for the court to formulate the criteria that would allow *the nine estates to be handled informally*. Furthermore, even if supervision is shown to be unnecessary in many cases, *perhaps it is this supervision that lessens or prevents problems such as dishonesty and carelessness.*

Sample Situation

Some have written that attorneys are made rich by the probate process. I have tried neither to praise nor criticize attorneys. However, as with all your concerns, you only have two sources of information: yourself and some trusted person. Some similar situations come to mind: if you want to sell your home, you can decide to seek the assistance of a *real estate broker* or sell it yourself; if you want to invest in the stock market, you can hire a *full-service brokerage firm* that advises you on your transactions or you can advise yourself (and just have a discount brokerage firm place your orders); if you are preparing your tax return, you can go to an *accountant* or you can do it yourself. No real estate manual, investment literature, tax return instruction guide, or book on wills can give you the clear and relevant advice that can be obtained from your own personal advisor. But some people decide not to seek personal professional help. Although independence is a sign of wonderful emotional maturity, *sometimes people do need assistance.*

Money-Saving Suggestions

How many copies of the letters testamentary should initially be ordered? Count the depositories holding assets of the deceased; each will require one copy. Do not order too many copies, however. Someone later on who seeks proof of your identity will require a copy that is recently dated. (This does not mean that probate is undertaken all over again. It just requires a trip to the courthouse to obtain a copy of the letters testamentary, stamped with the date of your trip; or telephone your attorney, who can obtain it quite readily.)

Another suggestion is to remember that the court can issue *preliminary letters testamentary*. Essentially it is permission granted to the executor named in a will, which has not yet been approved by the court, to *safeguard* the estate assets, but without the authority to *distribute* these assets to the legatees. This is useful in those situations where either the next of kin is being located or happens to be challenging the will.

THE COSTS OF DYING

The doctor's bill and the funeral bill are obvious costs of dying. There are also taxes. But there are other costs of dying. Probate results in the additional costs of the *court filing fee, the executor's bond, the attorney's fee, and the executor's fee.*

General estimates of these costs can be stated as a percentage of the value of the estate: the court filing fee and the executor's bond are less than one percent; the attorney's fee is approximately two to four percent; and the executor's fee is approximately three to four percent.

These administrative costs can be *avoided through joint ownership of assets with a right of survivorship.* But remember the problems of joint ownership: there may be a gift tax triggered at the time of the creation of the joint ownership; the joint asset is a target of creditors of either owner; if held jointly with a spouse, a divorce settlement may be affected by a joint ownership; if the intended joint ownership is not properly recorded as such, the asset will eventually be owned by distributees if there is no will.

Here is an example of this last problem. Margaret and Mary, who are sisters, have a joint certificate of deposit; upon expiration it is renewed, but (either mistakenly or deliberately) Mary's name is omitted. When Margaret dies, the certificate of deposit goes to the residuary legatee in her will. If Margaret has no will, the certificate of deposit goes to her distributees. This can prove to be quite unfortunate *if some undesirable relative is one of the distributees.*

Some people complain about the costs of probate and estate administration. Bear in mind, however, that the purposes of probate and estate administration are to evaluate any claims against the estate and then to distribute to the legatees the property of the deceased free of any claims of creditors. These purposes are important to both the *creditors* and the *legatees.* Therefore, it is a court-supervised estate and, yes, it is expensive. It is also time-consuming. But rather than having a society hell-bent on avoiding court supervision and its costs, in my opinion a better solution is to *streamline the whole process of probate and administration of an estate.*

Many states are reacting to the outcry that the legal costs of dying are too high. The best development so far is the previously mentioned streamlined procedure most states now have for the administration of smaller estates (a procedure similar to Small Claims Courts).

Sample Situation

Probate can be avoided by transferring all your assets to a trust. In many states you can be the trustee of the trust and also the beneficiary. You name a successor trustee who is to take your place upon your resignation (perhaps due to illness) or your death. *The trust instrument determines to whom the assets are to be distributed upon your death.* If you follow this approach, make sure all your assets are legally owned by the trust. (For example, John Jones's bank account would now be owned by the Revocable Grantor Trust of John Jones dated November 11, 1991.) Benefits of this trust are that you *retain control* of your assets, you *can revoke* the trust at any time, someone is there to handle your affairs if you cannot continue to be trustee, and there can be a *savings in probate costs* at the time of your death.

Note that the trust is *revocable:* you reserve the right to make changes. If it is not revocable, there can be problems. First of all, *you cannot change it.* Also, there is a *gift tax consequence* because you have made a gift (to take effect in the future) to those receiving the assets upon your death.

Should you set up this type of trust and avoid probate? The trade-off is that while the cost of the future probate might be reduced because the assets avoid probate, there is still the legal expense of establishing the trust. Also a trust is informal and assets will be transferred at the time of your death without court supervision. Proceed cautiously whether you set up a revocable or irrevocable trust, and sign the trust instrument only after it has been thoroughly explained and you understand it (*particularly the tax consequences*).

Money-Saving Suggestion

Unless you think your executor is an incompetent or a crook (and therefore you would not name this person), *why have the estate pay for an executor's bond?* A bond is a promise made to the court by a bonding company that it will pay any losses caused by the executor's negligence or dishonesty. The bond usually costs between a few hundred and a few thousand dollars, and this amount is saved by your estate if your will states that a bond is not necessary. It is a simple statement that can be expressed in your will quite clearly, like this: "My executor (or successor executor, if serving) shall not be required to post a bond in any jurisdiction." This waiver of the bond does not lower the standard of care required by an executor. He or she is still required to be honest and competent, which is the subject of chapter 15.

In the next chapter, we will explore the gathering of assets, particularly the deceased's safe deposit box; the deceased's business; and the deceased's home and its contents.

13

Gathering Assets

GATHER, APPRAISE, AND SAFEGUARD

In most situations, it is easy to gather the deceased's assets. They consist of furniture, clothing, jewelry, household articles, and money. Perhaps the assets also include a house, an automobile, the value of a life insurance policy if owned by the deceased (and without regard to whom it is payable or whose life is insured), and employee benefits. Gathering the assets usually presents no major problems, although some assets are more obvious than others. One not so obvious asset is any legal claim that the deceased, if still alive, could assert; perhaps it is a claim against the person who caused the death (e.g., the driver of an automobile). Another less obvious asset is insurance reimbursement for medical expenses paid by the deceased. One problem in gathering assets is encountered in every estate: *How is the executor sure that all the assets have been gathered?* He or she must go through all the deceased's papers, thoroughly search the house, look at recent tax returns, and review all mail sent to the deceased after death. The ideal situation occurs, of course, when the *deceased has left the inventory of assets that I have so often stressed throughout this book.*

An appraisal of some assets may be needed. Real estate, works of art, furniture, and jewelry are four examples of items requiring appraisal. To have a record of the value of decedent's *shares of corporate stock* at the time of death, consult the *Wall Street Journal.*

Most importantly, immediately following the death, the personal representative of the estate must *safeguard* these assets until they are

119

distributed. If the deceased lived alone, change the lock on the apartment or house. Be sure that home-owner's or tenant insurance is still in force. Deposit the money assets you gather, such as bank accounts, in an interest-bearing estate account and be sure that the estate account is protected by the Federal Deposit Insurance Corporation (F.D.I.C.). If the estate account exceeds the maximum amount covered by the F.D.I.C., then invest the excess amount in United States Treasury Department securities (preferably the short-term bills so that the money is quickly available for distribution). If the estate owns corporate stock, exercise extreme caution. Ideally, the assets should be distributed as quickly as possible.

Sample Situations

In gathering assets, I send the following letter to banks where the deceased might have had an account:

> As the attorney for the Estate of Michael Testator, I represent Michael Testator, Jr., the Executor, and enclose his certificate of Letters Testamentary. Also enclosed is a notice from your bank, found in the home of the deceased, that refers to account #500681. Please give me a written response to these four questions:
>
> What was the balance in account #500681 on (give date of death)?
>
> Is any other name listed on this account? If so, advise me if there is a right of survivorship and provide me with documentation.
>
> Are there any certificates of deposit or other accounts in Michael Testator's name? If so, what are the account numbers and balances as of (date of death)? Are any other names listed on these accounts and, if so, is there a right of survivorship?
>
> Is there a safe deposit box?

You should always include the question on the existence of a safe deposit box. Sometimes a person has more than one safe deposit box, so be on the lookout for a second or even a third such depository by following my earlier suggestions with respect to reviewing the deceased's cancelled checks for the previous year, and by asking each bank that has money assets of the deceased. Also, do not assume that a bank will automatically notify you of the existence of a safe deposit box; you must ask this question.

In collecting money assets, it has been my experience that telephone calls and exchange of correspondence with the bank or brokerage firm are not the best methods of communication. If possible, *go to the depository.* Personal contact, whenever possible, results in a faster and more efficient gathering of assets.

Money-Saving Suggestion

A suggestion to executors, relatives, and friends of the deceased: do not go through the deceased's papers and other personal items *without a witness.* This avoids the accusation that you stole money, jewelry, or other items of value.

THE SAFE DEPOSIT BOX

Even if there are joint owners of the safe deposit box, the survivor is not allowed access to it. *The law of most states directs that the safe deposit box of a deceased person is to be sealed.* It is to be opened only by the personal representative of the estate who, in many states, is accompanied by a representative of the state's taxation department.

One way that a surviving owner of a safe deposit box can illegally gain access is by pretending that nothing has happened to the now deceased co-owner. Another subterfuge is to have a box, held in the name of a corporation, contain assets owned by an individual; upon the individual's death, a surviving corporate officer can gain access. I do not advise either tactic. The "let's get to the box" attitude is motivated by an attempt to escape estate taxation. It usually results in tax evasion of an inconsequential amount that is usually less than the *value placed on the energy that went into this improper activity.*

Cash should not be stored in a safe deposit box. First, if cash is discovered by a taxation official, an income tax might be levied upon this asset. Why? Because the taxation official might presume that tax evasion has occurred. Second, someone in a cash business who evades tax and stores the cash in a safe deposit box is losing the investment income this money would yield. This income from investments would soon exceed the amount of income tax evaded.

Here is the major problem with joint ownership of the safe deposit box. Suppose the survivor of the two owners gets to the bank *after* the bank has discovered the death of the other owner. The safe deposit box will have already been sealed. Then, when the state tax official inventories the box, the *survivor's items* in the box, along with the deceased's items in the box, are presumed to be the property of the deceased's estate. This can result in a higher estate tax. If you do share a safe deposit box, then have a note in the box, signed by both owners, stating who owns what.

In times past, safe deposit boxes were quite popular because bonds payable to the bearer were an investment held by many people. Upon the owner's death, the heir (or a thief) would go to the box and become the new bearer, and estate tax was thereby evaded. Today, bearer bonds are virtually nonexistent. A safe deposit box should be used to *safeguard your valuable items,* and not for the purpose of *tax evasion.*

Sample Situation

A safe deposit box is not the best place for important papers such as your burial instructions or a cemetery deed. If you want to be cremated, or if you have other instructions that need immediate action, make sure these instructions are known by someone who cares, and that the instructions are not hidden away in a safe deposit box. *The safe deposit box will not be opened in time to fulfill your wishes.* Perhaps you are aware of cases where these situations occurred, and how frustration and guilt resulted because the dead person's wishes were not fulfilled. Spare your family and friends the embarrassment of finding out too late what your last wishes were regarding the disposal of your physical remains.

If all your important papers, including burial instructions, are in your safe deposit box, here is a way to avoid the case of the *cremation that did not occur.* Keep *photocopies* of these papers at home and, most importantly, tell someone (your executor is a good choice) of your wishes.

Money-Saving Suggestions

Rather than two people jointly owning a safe deposit box, I suggest they rent separate ones. However, each can have a *power of attorney* for the other's safe deposit box. Consider this example: Mary and Sue each has her own safe deposit box and each has a power of attorney for the other person's box. If either one of them is sick and unable to go to their respective safe deposit boxes, the other one can go even though she is not a co-owner. Then, when either Sue or Mary dies, *only one safe deposit box is sealed.* The survivor's is unknown to the tax authorities. This suggestion is preferable to what often happens: two people have a jointly held safe deposit box; their jewelry, cash, bearer bonds (if any), and other items are in the one box; the survivor is to go to the box as soon as possible; however, the grieving survivor forgets to do this and the box is sealed by the bank. The tax authority then claims that all the items in the safe deposit box were owned by the deceased person.

A final suggestion deals with the *need* for a safe deposit box. Unfortunately, due to the prospect of burglary, such a precaution is needed to safeguard valuable items, including legal documents and jewelry. Consider whether or not you have a need for a safe deposit box. *Most people do need one.*

THE DECEASED'S BUSINESS

The owner(s) of a business, including partnerships and corporations, should plan for the inevitability of death. It is a good idea for the owners to discuss with each other the consequences of the death of either or all of them. If the business has only one owner, this owner should educate a successor or two, and thus assure the continuation of the business after the owner's death.

What happens to a business when the owner dies? The personal representative of the estate continues the business until it is transferred to the new owner. It is an important job, because the business may be the most valuable asset in the estate.

Here are five suggestions I give to a personal representative of the estate in such situations: (1) *Read the deceased's will* to find out if there are any instructions concerning the business. (2) Remember that you *act at your peril* in continuing the business. (3) Continue the business only until you are legally able to *transfer it* to the person or persons who inherited it. (4) *Consult with the eventual owners* before each and every decision regarding the business. (5) Do not use *other assets of the estate* to pay any expenses of the business.

Perhaps the executor is authorized by the will to sell the business. If so, be sure that a qualified appraiser establishes the company's value. The executor should invite input from the legatees before a contract of sale is signed. Give the legatees an opportunity to bid more for the business than the prospective buyer has offered. Also, be sure that there are no other interested buyers who are willing to offer more than the price you are about to accept.

If a business is sold after the death of the owner, then most likely *the deceased had not adequately planned for the eventuality of death.* The product of a lifetime of hard work should not be terminated by death, but should be continued by a legatee chosen and trained by the owner.

Sample Situations

There are many cases of a small business losing all its value during the administration of an estate. If the testator has not trained a successor, and if the personal representative of the estate is not a good manager, then chaos results.

During the administration of an estate, a business can lose its value for a variety of reasons, including: loss of *customers,* loss of *employees,* loss of *suppliers,* a lost *lease,* and lost (or stolen) *inventory.* Whether a business is to be continued by an heir or eventually sold, it is the job of the personal representative of the estate to preserve its value during the administration of the estate.

Whether to sell or keep the business is too broad a question on which to generalize. *Keep in mind that retaining the business might be the riskier choice,* when compared to the stability of conservatively investing the proceeds from the sale of the business. On the other hand, it is sad to see it sold if the reason for the sale is that *no one knows how to run the business.*

Money-Saving Suggestion

Owners of a business should acquaint themselves with a buy-sell agreement. The co-owners might decide among themselves the value of each owner's interest in the company, and agree that, upon the death of an owner, the deceased owner's share is to be acquired by the other owner(s). The cost of this acquisition can be funded by life insurance.

In the situation where *there is only one owner of the business,* an arrangement might be made with a prospective buyer, perhaps an employee. An agreed upon value of the business is determined, and upon the owner's death the business is sold. *Be sure to update annually any agreement that states the value of the business.*

A benefit of such an agreement—perhaps the best benefit of all— is that it forces an owner to *plan for the consequences of death.* Be aware,

however, that your personal advisor must grapple with the tax consequences, particularly the effect of Section 2036(c) of the Internal Revenue
Code (which is beyond the scope of this volume).

THE HOUSE AND ITS CONTENTS

Here is a warning to the personal representative of the estate and close
relatives: *do not discard anything* without first giving serious thought to
its possible value. What appears to you to have little or no value may
have great value to some other person. If that other person is to inherit
what you just discarded, then you are in trouble. Have witnesses, and
ask the legatees for input. *Also, do not overlook anything.* Look carefully
in drawers, under the mattress, and in places where the deceased may
have hidden something; sometimes you can find hidden treasures. These
hidden treasures, of course, will be part of the estate and not the property
of the finder. Be optimistic: search the attic because that is where the
old paintings, first editions, and antiques are found. *Old does not mean
worthless, whether it is a painting, a book, an antique, or a person.*

If the deceased lived alone, whether in an apartment or a private
home, I again advise you to be sure that the dwelling is insured and secured. Be sure that jewelry and other valuable items are removed from
the dwelling before the moving company arrives. The post office should
be advised to forward mail to the personal representative of the estate.
Make sure no one other than the personal representative of the estate
or a chosen family member is allowed access to the dwelling. As for the
furniture of a deceased person who lived alone, perhaps the person who
inherits the furniture wants to donate some or all of it to a charity. Similarly,
the person who inherits the clothing may also want to donate it to a
charity. If there is a lease to an apartment occupied by a deceased who
lived alone, the attorney for the estate can advise on the possibility of
terminating it. Alternatively, the continuation of a favorable lease can be
a valuable asset of the estate (and this is the subject of the next sample
situation).

As for the accumulated mail and other miscellaneous papers, I recommend that after they are reviewed, retain them. Hidden among these
assorted papers may be a will, the address of a next of kin, a bank statement, a letter from a creditor that a debt was cancelled or paid, a suggestion of the location of a safe deposit box, a deed, a lease, or some other
important document. When the estate is closed, undertake a final review

of these papers. If need be, at this time *they can be discarded.* Why hoard papers that have no worth? If you are in doubt as to what you should retain, consult with the attorney for the estate.

Sample Situation

The rent a landlord charges on an apartment is controlled in some communities by the local government. This often results in a rent that is *significantly less* than what it would be in a free enterprise system, where rent is set at whatever the market will bear. Rent control protects senior citizens living on a fixed income, and in such instances it is a wonderful idea. I oppose it when wealthy individuals, of whatever age, reap its benefits.

A result of this *rent control* is the situation of a family member who *claims to have been living in the apartment and therefore should be allowed to continue renting it at an artificially low rent.* Sometimes this is a valid claim. But whether the landlord or the tenant should prevail is not as important as my concern that the personal representative of the estate does *not quickly surrender possession of the apartment.* Find out what choices the law allows, what the interested family members want to do, and then make your decision. A premature surrender of the lease may turn out to be the *surrender of the estate's most valuable asset.*

Money-Saving Suggestions

Suppose you inherit your aunt's furniture, and further suppose that you have no use for it. I suggest that this used but usable furniture can be given to a charity. Both you and the charity are richer for this gift, and you do not have to wait long for your reward—just until April 15th when you list the value of this gift as an income tax deduction. An asset received from an estate has a date-of-death value for tax purposes, and this is the value placed on a charitable gift of the asset. So be sure that the furniture is appraised for these two reasons: it is needed for the *estate tax return,* and it is needed to substantiate the amount of the charitable deduction taken on the *individual income tax return* of someone who has made a charitable gift of property received from an estate.

I further suggest that you consider *disclaiming* this legacy, perhaps to allow your successor, who then receives it, to give it to a charity. Your decision depends on whether you or the successor legatee is in the higher income tax bracket; that is, which of you has the greater income tax savings as a result of the charitable gift. But balance this tax advice with the practical decision as to whether you want someone to get richer at your expense. Let us now take a closer look at this technique called *disclaimer* and learn who receives a legacy that has been disclaimed.

14

Distributing Assets

REFUSING AN INHERITANCE (DISCLAIMER)

A person is allowed to refuse a legacy, or to refuse a portion of a legacy. This is called *disclaimer,* or *partial disclaimer.* Why does someone disclaim? Perhaps there is a successor legatee named, and the person disclaiming wants this successor legatee to receive the legacy. For example, suppose James is entitled to receive a legacy of $50,000, and the deceased's will further states: "If James has predeceased me, this $50,000 goes to his son, John." If James disclaims the legacy, he is considered to have predeceased the testator, and his son, John, then receives the legacy.

But why would James want his son John to receive the legacy? One reason might be that James is *terribly in debt;* he knows that if he accepts the $50,000, then his creditors will quickly grab it. Another reason might be that James is *rich* and old, and his eventual estate faces a high estate tax. By disclaiming this legacy, he passes this property on to his son, without the property eventually being included in his own estate. Caution must be taken that the disclaimer is properly made, so as not to be treated as a gift made by the person disclaiming the legacy to the person receiving the legacy, and thereby subject to a gift tax (which you will learn about in Part Three).

Notice that in my example *there is a successor legatee named in the will.* If no successor legatee is named, then the disclaimed legacy *goes to the residuary legatee(s) or their successors.* If they also disclaim, then the distributees receive the disclaimed legacy. But even a distributee can disclaim. If this occurs, the other distributees receive the disclaimed legacy.

If you are thinking of disclaiming a legacy, be aware of the *time period* in which your state requires that a disclaimer must be made, and also be aware of the *identity* of the lucky recipient of what you disclaim.

A disclaimer is a *post-mortem estate planning tool.* Perhaps something is *overlooked* when the testator's will is prepared; alternatively, something happens *after* the will is prepared. But if there is to be an oversight, it is always better to have one that can be corrected. It is also possible that some post-mortem planning is not a corrective measure; it merely implements an idea that was not relevant prior to the testator's death, *but is now relevant, perhaps due to a change in the legatee's life.*

Sample Situations

Any estate asset received by a surviving spouse is *free of federal estate tax* (but only if the surviving spouse is a United States citizen). Therefore, the child of a decedent might choose to disclaim a legacy if the surviving parent would then become the recipient of the legacy. *This avoids estate tax.* For example, if a husband leaves one-half of his estate to his wife and the other half to his child, then the child might elect to receive only so much of the legacy that is free of estate tax and disclaim the balance. This occurs only in estates of substantial value (as you will learn in Part Three, up to $600,000 worth of assets—in addition to any assets received by a surviving spouse—can pass free of federal estate tax). But if the father leaves an estate of *$2 million equally to his wife and his child,* perhaps the *child might disclaim* $400,000. The child then receives $600,000 (and this amount is free of estate tax), and the surviving spouse receives $1,400,000 (which is also tax free).

Sometimes the reverse situation occurs. Suppose a husband and wife are each worth $1 million. If the husband dies first and has left *everything* to his wife, perhaps the *wife might disclaim* $600,000. Whether or not she disclaims, there is no estate tax on the husband's estate. But the wife knows there is going to be a substantial estate tax *on her eventual estate.* If her children are the successor legatees, she might decide to disclaim, and have some of the assets now pass *directly from the husband's estate to the children, thus avoiding eventual inclusion in her taxable estate.*

Money-Saving Suggestion

You have learned that a disclaimer can save taxes, or it can protect money from the creditor(s) of a legatee. But the legatee who is contemplating a disclaimer must make a practical decision. Is the tax that is saved or the creditor's claim that is avoided *worth the loss of the legacy?* The child of the wealthy deceased person may decide to accept the legacy, even if it results in the payment by the estate of an estate tax. The child has no assurance that the surviving parent will reward a tax-wise disclaimer. (In fact, a too obvious reward, such as an immediate gift to the disclaiming person, may disqualify the tax benefit of the disclaimer.) So, too, a debt-ridden legatee may decide to accept the legacy, pay off the creditor, and face the world without the burden of a stalking creditor. The question of whether or not to disclaim is a difficult one to answer. *Once disclaimed, the legacy cannot be reclaimed.*

PRELIMINARY CONSIDERATIONS

After the assets of an estate have been gathered, it is then time for the personal representative of the estate to distribute them. Here are some considerations:

> *Early distribution* should be the goal. This is a courtesy to those who are to receive the property. Remember to obtain a receipt from the recipient of an estate distribution. Also, remember to retain sufficient assets to pay any debts of the estate that might eventually be incurred.

> Find out if an advancement of a legacy has been made by the deceased. An *advancement* is a gift that was made by the now deceased person, with the intention that the gift reduces what the recipient would other-wise receive as a legacy. If an advancement of a legacy was made by a deceased, the personal representative of the estate *must* reduce the legacy by the amount of the advancement.

> Where any real property (land, a house, or other buildings) is an estate asset, the *real property is sold* only *in extraordinary circumstances.* A situation where it could be sold is where there is insufficient cash to pay a creditor of the estate. However, even in this situation, the person entitled to the real property has the opportunity to take the property and reimburse the estate. A quick example of this situation:

Mary leaves her house, worth $100,000, to nephew John; Mary dies with no other assets and $10,000 of unpaid bills. John has the right to take the house and pay the estate $10,000.

If a *legatee has predeceased* the person whose estate is being administered, be certain as to what happens to this legacy. It may go to the *surviving children* (or grandchildren) of the predeceased legatee, and this situation can occur *when the predeceased legatee is closely related to the decedent,* such as a legacy left to the testator's now predeceased brother.

If you are the personal representative of an estate, you should review with your attorney any problem about the distribution of assets *before* making the distribution. If an item has been improperly distributed, it may be hard to retrieve; if money has been improperly distributed, it might have been spent by the recipient who now has no money to make repayment.

A legacy of a *specific item* carries with it any *increase* in the item's value. However, a bequest of money earns interest only in some state jurisdictions. This is the subject of the sample situation.

Sample Situation

Suppose a legatee is left $10,000. Does the legatee receive interest income on the $10,000? In many states the legatee does not earn interest income on the legacy. However, in some states a legacy does earn this interest income, but not until after a specific period of time has elapsed (approximately one year) from the date of death. Where interest on the legacy is required to be paid, *it is paid even if the personal representative of the estate has not invested the deceased's money,* and the amount is based on the prevailing rate of interest. For the oversight of not investing the estate assets, the personal representative of the estate is *surcharged,* which means making payment from his or her own funds to the estate for the loss incurred. This will occur even if the executor *does not know that estate assets should be prudently invested.* The executor is *still liable* (as you will learn in chapter 15 in the discussion on liability of the personal representative).

Money-Saving Suggestions

You may receive income from your legacy in either of two situations. The first situation I just described: there is an inordinate delay in receiving the legacy and the legatee receives interest on this legacy. The second, and much more frequently encountered situation, is the *receipt by the residuary legatee(s) of the income*—including interest or dividend income not otherwise paid to another legatee—that was earned while the estate was being administered.

I suggest that if you do receive income from the legacy, then fulfill your obligation to *pay any income tax that is due on it.* (Do not confuse *income* from a legacy and a *legacy*—you do not pay any *income tax* on the *legacy itself.*) Just as your employer sends to you and the government a W-2 form that states your taxable wages, and just as your bank sends to you and the government a 1099 form that states your taxable bank account interest income, the executor sends to you and the government a K-1 form. *This form states the taxable amount of interest, dividends, and other income that you have received from the estate.* Unlike the small W-2 and 1099 forms, the K-1 form is a full-size sheet of paper.

I have two suggestions concerning any K-1 form you might receive. First, *report as taxable income* on your individual income tax return the amount stated on the K-1 form as taxable to you. This you should do not only to fulfill your obligations as a citizen, but also to avoid the assessment of interest and penalties on any tax assessment on this income. Second, you may have a *deduction* stated on the K-1 form, so be sure you take advantage of this deduction on your individual income tax return.

TOO FEW ASSETS

Ademption and *abatement* are legal terms often used when discussing an estate. They describe situations in which the optimistic deceased leaves more through the will than is eventually available to be distributed. The easiest way to explain these words is through examples.

Suppose Grandmother's will provides that Mary is to receive all her General Motors stock. After signing her will, however, Grandmother sells the stock, and upon her death there is no General Motors stock among the estate assets. This is an example of *ademption,* which simply means that a legatee would have gotten something if it were there to get. The legatee does not get it, however, because the *deceased did not own it at the time of death.* Not too much has to be discussed about ademption. If you leave a specific item to someone, and then you dispose of the item, you may want to have a new will prepared and leave some other item to the person whose legacy has been lost through ademption.

Now a few words about abatement. Suppose that Grandmother's will provides that person A is to receive $20,000, person B is to receive $40,000, and person C is to receive $60,000. Grandmother dies and leaves an estate of only $60,000, despite her optimism that her net worth would be $120,000 at death. Through abatement, person A receives $10,000, person B receives $20,000, and person C receives $30,000. *Abatement* simply means *a proportional reduction* in each legacy when the estate has insufficient assets to pay all the legacies.

To avoid abatement, you should clearly express in your will the priority of legacies. If you are leaving money to a number of people, you can express your desire as to which legacies are to be paid first. Therefore, if your net worth declines, your will has covered this situation, and the preferred legacies are not reduced by abatement. Another way of avoiding abatement is to use a *fractional formula* in the residuary clause. In the above example, Grandmother really wants to leave *one-sixth* to person A, *two-sixths* to person B, and *three-sixths* to person C. Perhaps this is the preferred way for Grandmother to express her intent, rather than by giving specific amounts to the three legatees.

Sample Situations

It is confusing to read legalese, the technical language of attorneys. Ideas should be expressed in understandable language. Imagine an attorney telling a person who had been bequeathed $60,000 by Grandmother's will that this amount is now *subject to an abatement.* The person's immediate thought might be that this abatement is a bonus. The person will be enraged when told that the legacy is to be reduced. An attorney's scholarly lecture on the legal development of the abatement doctrine will only heighten the rage.

I present these legal terms, ademption and abatement, not only because of their impact on estates, but also to show you that *the ideas expressed in the administration of an estate are not extremely complex.* Word usage, however, sometimes makes the subject difficult. Estate planning, estate administration, and taxation should be expressed in plain language whenever possible, because they are subjects of importance to everyone. Legislators and attorneys should heed this advice.

Money-Saving Suggestions

Some of you really like the idea of leaving your shares of stock in General Motors or AT&T to your legatees, so here is another idea.

Suppose you own General Motors stock that is now worth $50,000, and you want your favorite niece to receive it. In order to protect your niece's legacy in the event you sell your General Motors stock or it declines dramatically in value, I suggest you consider the following. Leave her all the shares of General Motors stock you might own at the time of your death, but add: "If the value of this stock is less than $50,000 at that time, I leave her a cash bequest of the amount by which $50,000 exceeds the value of all my shares of General Motors stock." Therefore, if the General Motors stock is worth $30,000 when you die, your niece will receive this stock plus $20,000. If your General Motors stock is worth $100,000, then that is what your niece receives. *This suggestion might save you the cost of having a new will or codicil prepared.*

On the other hand, maybe you just want to leave her the General Motors stock. If you do not own it at your death, then she doesn't receive it; or if you do own it but it is only worth $30,000, then that's what she receives. *You decide.* These are just various *options available to you.*

Here is another thought on this subject. I am sure there are readers who have wills that leave shares of stock in the AT&T Corporation to someone, and these wills were written before the federal government reorganized AT&T. Do you want the legatee to receive the shares of stock in the spin-off Baby Bell Corporations? Your will should be updated if you want the legatee to receive the spin-off corporation shares; otherwise, *NYNEX and her orphan sisters might go to the residuary legatee.*

CREDITORS OF THE ESTATE

The distribution of the deceased's assets is made to the legatees and the creditors of the estate. Paying the creditors is a major job of the personal representative of the estate, and it is more complex than distributing the legacies. The creditors of the estate include those who are owed money *by the deceased* and also those who are owed money *by the estate.*

Two likely creditors of the estate are the *doctor* who treated the deceased during the final illness and the *funeral home.* Many times these bills are paid by close family members who then become the creditors of the estate. The personal representative of the estate should reimburse these people, but only after receiving proof of payment of the medical bills and the funeral bill.

Other major creditors of the estate are the *tax collectors*. As you will learn in Part Three, the taxes could be for the *current year's federal and state income tax,* or perhaps tax owed on *prior years' income* (due to an audit or maybe tax returns were never filed), or the *federal and state income tax on the income generated by the estate during its administration,* or any *estate taxes*.

Keep in mind that the personal representative of the estate can be personally liable to the creditors of the estate. This can occur if *all the assets of the deceased are distributed to the legatees before the legitimate creditors of the estate are paid*. In this instance, the *creditors* can sue the personal representative of the estate. The personal representative is also in trouble if *debts that are NOT legally enforceable ARE paid;* in this instance, the *legatees* can sue the personal representative of the estate.

The personal representative should read the will; sometimes it contains information regarding a decedent's debts.

Personal representatives should be on the lookout for fraudulent creditors. Occasionally the media report on bogus bills sent to a deceased with a claim that services were rendered or products were sold to the decedent. *Beware*.

In some states, the *creditors* are required, within a specified time period, to file a notice of claim; in other states, the *personal representative of the estate* needs to publish a notice of his appointment. Through these procedures, the personal representative of the estate is alerted to the existence of claims. In practice, however, the personal representative usually becomes aware of the deceased's debts *through the receipt of bills mailed to the deceased's last known address*.

Sample Situation

A creditor claims he is owed money by the deceased, but there is no solid evidence of this debt. Although not certain of the validity of the claim, the personal representative of the estate pays the debt. The residuary legatee then sues the personal representative. The result might be a *surcharge* and, as you know, this means the personal representative is required to reimburse the estate for the cost of the error. In this case, the amount of the surcharge would be the *amount erroneously paid to the creditor*.

These sad cases always occur. If you are the personal representative of an estate, do not pay claims of creditors unless you are *absolutely certain that there is a legal obligation to pay*. On this your attorney can advise you.

Money-Saving Suggestions

In some situations it is advisable to settle a creditor's questionable claim. This suggestion should be considered with an awareness of the *costs of litigation that can be avoided if a claim is settled*. This compromise should be approved either by the court or the legatees—ideally, by both. Until such time as the situation is resolved, the personal representative of the estate must retain in the estate account an amount equal to the amount of the claim. If all the assets of the estate have been distributed and the creditor then prevails in its claim against the estate, the personal representative of the estate is most likely *personally liable* for payment.

For *creditors of an estate*, here is a suggested statement of a claim, precise and uncomplicated, filed by a creditor: "To the Estate of John Testator: there is due to me from the Estate of John Testator the sum of $3,000, for medical services rendered to John Testator during the two months preceding his death." Have your attorney review this statement, serve it upon the estate, and file it in court.

15

Final Thoughts on Estate Administration

LIABILITY OF THE PERSONAL REPRESENTATIVE

In fulfilling the wishes of the deceased as expressed in the will, *the personal representative of the estate should not attempt to implement personal ideas as to what is fair.* Ask the attorney for the estate to advise you on the proper legal solution to a problem. The personal representative is liable for mistakes made in administering the estate, so be careful. Let us review a few of the areas where caution should be exercised.

Make sure that all *tax audits have been completed* before distributing all the estate assets. You can ask the Internal Revenue Service to expedite its review of tax returns. If an audit determines that tax is owed, and *assets which could have been available for taxes have been distributed,* then the personal representative of the estate *might* be liable for the payment of the tax.

Caution must be exercised in the areas of *sale of assets* and *payment of claims.* If it is necessary to sell any asset of the estate, then the representative is required to obtain the best possible price and to substantiate why this price is the best possible price obtainable. Appraisals by experts, bidding, and comparable sales are ways to meet this requirement of price substantiation. As for payment of claims, *do not pay* any claim against the estate unless you are certain that there is a legal obligation to pay. On the other hand, make sure that you *do pay* the claims of the estate that are legally enforceable against it.

Receive consents from interested parties, whenever possible, regarding those difficult decisions pertaining to the distribution of assets. A decision is difficult when there exists the possibility that a reasonable person could question your judgment. I know this advice is vague, but an executor needs his or her own attorney to render an opinion on the variety of problems that can arise with respect to asset distribution, and what decisions by an executor a "reasonable person could question."

Also *receive a final release,* signed by each legatee, attesting that the distribution of assets has been made. To the residuary legatee's release, attach *a copy of your accounting* of all the estate funds that you received and disbursed (otherwise, the person signing the release may claim that he or she was not fully informed). Receive the release (and the approval of the accounting from the residuary legatees) before the legacy is distributed.

The personal representative of the estate cannot delegate to others the jobs entailed in administering an estate; it is a hands-on operation. Clerical tasks obviously can be delegated. But I cannot overemphasize that each decision involved in handling estate assets has to be made by the personal representative, because he or she is answerable to any claimant for each decision.

Sample Situation

There are cases where the personal representative of the estate is criticized, sued, and surcharged for being too extravagant. This occurs when the funeral costs are excessive or payments are made to questionable creditors. Be careful, and consult the attorney for the estate frequently during the administration of the estate. The personal representative, whether as executor or as administrator, is personally liable for errors made and may be *required by the court to reimburse the estate for these errors.*

The standard that is demanded of the personal representative is a *reasonable business person's standard of care: how a reasonably smart business person would handle a similar situation.* If this general level of care is not achieved, then watch out. Surcharge may result. Being a personal representative can be a rewarding job, financially and emotionally. But it is difficult. Be careful, honest, and thorough; *things will work out all right.*

Money-Saving Suggestion

The most costly mistake a personal representative of the estate can make (although often undetected) is not collecting all the deceased's assets. In many cases elderly people are circumspect about how much or how little they have. Sometimes they are downright misleading. Therefore, do not rely on a testator's sympathy-evoking statement that there will *not be much in my estate.* There might be a whole lot in the estate, so search thoroughly.

Furthermore, the personal representative should use a *checklist* to avoid careless oversights that might lead to a lawsuit. The result of this lawsuit might be that the personal representative reaches into his or her own pocket, removes money, and gives it to the estate. How much money is given to the estate? It is the amount that the court determines is fair restitution for losses caused by carelessness or extravagance.

A CHECKLIST FOR THE PERSONAL REPRESENTATIVE

The job of the personal representative of the estate, whether as an executor or an administrator, is all-encompassing. Here is a summary of the personal representative's responsibilities:

Secure the home; arrange the funeral; order the death certificates.

Arrange for the mail of the deceased to be held at the post office, and upon your appointment as the personal representative, have the mail forwarded to you.

Locate the will. Select the attorney to represent the estate, unless it is a small, uncomplicated estate that you have decided to handle yourself.

Review all the insurance policies of the deceased; suggest to the survivors that they review their own insurance policies.

Contact the employer of the deceased (or the former employer of a retiree) and learn what death benefits are owed to the estate.

Send a copy of the will to any interested party who requests it. (However, do not remove the staples from the will when photocopying it.)

Locate all the next of kin. Do not be secretive with any legatees or next of kin.

Review all the deceased's records in order to determine the assets and the liabilities of the estate.

Gather all the assets; enter the safe deposit box; and continue running the deceased's business, if necessary.

Obtain an appraisal of property.

Notify the Social Security Administration of the death.

Review the tax returns for the three years prior to death.

Determine the rights of creditors.

Open up an estate checking account.

Pay all estate taxes and all income taxes.

Sell assets, but only if this is allowable and necessary.

Distribute all the legacies.

Receive releases from all the legatees.

File the accounting in court, if necessary, and then your job is over.

The personal representative of the estate needs the advice of an experienced estate attorney, particularly in the areas of obtaining court appointment, paying taxes, resolving adverse claims, distributing assets, and filing an accounting. This might not be necessary, however, in a small, uncomplicated estate. The trick is to estimate accurately, at the outset, the *size and complexity of the estate* (which, once again, could be made infinitely easier if an asset inventory were available).

Sample Situation

I am aware of an estate in which nothing has been done in the two years since the date of death. The court, legatees, creditors, and taxation authorities have been exceptionally quiet. Any year now there will be a crisis, and most likely it will be precipitated by the Internal Revenue Service, looking for income tax returns. The case of the lazy personal representative is a sad one because when things heat up, *the job is a nightmare.* Therefore, if you are a personal representative of an estate and cannot handle the job, then go to court and obtain permission to resign. Do not put this off just because your inactivity has not yet been questioned. At some point it will be questioned, and then you will have a *major problem on your hands.*

Money-Saving Suggestion

Prior to your appointment as the personal representative of an estate, do not sign any contracts on behalf of the estate. If a contract must be signed, then it must be conditioned on being ratified after your appointment as executor or administrator. There also should be an express provision in the contract that you have not yet been appointed as the personal representative of the estate, and that you are not personally liable for the performance of the obligations stated in the contract. This was mentioned at the outset of Part Two in the discussion of the agreement made with an attorney prior to an individual's official appointment as executor. This suggestion applies to *all agreements* entered into by a named executor not yet appointed.

With regard to handling money: buy a simple ledger book and record in it every dollar you *receive* and every dollar you *spend*. Then buy two manila envelopes: in one, file proof of assets received, such as closed-out bank account books; in the other, file bills paid and receipts for payment. It is uncomplicated if you follow these suggestions. When the estate is ready to be wrapped up, the information for your accounting is efficiently organized. The main reasons for problems in preparing an accounting are (1) *the failure to record a transaction* and (2) *the failure to save documentation.* Accounting for money received and paid out is the major responsibility of the personal representative of the estate.

As for your other responsibilities, prepare a checklist. I offer this suggestion because I know that more mistakes are made by a personal representative who knows something has to be done but *forgets* to do it, than by a personal representative who does *not know* that something has to be done.

At the end of Part One you were presented with a long list of important documents and personal information that should be *located and safeguarded* at the time your will is prepared, and you have just reviewed a checklist for the *personal representative of an estate.* Now let us look at some *general reminders applicable to all who have a will prepared.*

A CHECKLIST FOR EVERYBODY

Does your executor know *where your will is located?* Does your executor know the names and addresses of your *next of kin?*

Do you have a *living will?* Does your doctor know you have it? Does a trusted person, such as your executor, know you have it?

Does your executor know if you have a *safe deposit box?* Does the executor know *where it is located?*

Have you discussed *funeral arrangements* with your executor or some other person close to you? If you own a cemetery plot, do you have the *deed?*

Do you know what property of yours is held in *joint ownership* with right of survivorship, and what bank accounts are *in trust for* someone?

Are all the insurance policies you own, bank accounts, and other investments included on *your inventory?* Do you know whether you have named someone as the beneficiary upon your death, or have you decided to have these assets distributed as part of your probate estate?

Is your Individual Retirement Account (IRA) included on your inventory? Do you have more than one account? Have you named someone as the beneficiary of these accounts upon your death? Alternatively, you might have decided that these accounts are to be distributed as part of your probate estate.

Do you know the death benefits provided by your *employer,* or *previous employer,* if retired, *and who will receive them?*

Is it clear which state is your *domiciliary state?* If you have real estate in another state, have you decided whether or not to name a joint owner with the right of survivorship so as to avoid ancillary probate in that state?

Do you have your *tax returns* (and supporting data) for the last three years?

Sample Situation

Your survivors will miss you, and they might not be emotionally able to sort through mountains of papers that have accumulated in your closets and drawers over the years. *Try to make things easy for them.*

The doubts of those who survive disorganized testators are consistent and constant: What were the wishes of the deceased? Were annual income tax returns filed? Did the deceased have a life insurance policy? Were out-of-state investments owned by the deceased? Where did the deceased want the family heirloom to go? Did the deceased have many debts? Did the deceased have a will, a safe deposit box, or a receipt for prepayment of funeral expenses? *What else should be done?* This agonizing can be extremely troublesome to those you love. If you have organized your estate, the burden of the personal representative will be significantly lighter.

Money-Saving Suggestion

Here is a summary of good reasons for having your affairs in order:

to make *your life* easier;

to assure that you and your possessions are adequately *insured;*

to clarify whether or not your cash assets are properly *invested;*

to secure the future of your *business;*

to assure that your assets are not *lost,* and thereby given to your state;

to help you (or, after your death, your executor) survive a *tax audit;*

to avoid the misfortune of the personal representative of your eventual estate paying a *debt* that you did not owe, or failing to collect a *debt owed to you;*

to lessen the cost of *probate;*

to assist your executor because, if you are organized, your estate will be *easier to administer.*

Put your affairs in order today!

PSYCHOLOGICAL ASPECTS

Let us conclude our journey through the administration of an estate by spending a few minutes on the psychological aspects of death. Those who lose a loved one experience shock, grief, and maybe guilt. But most of all the biggest hurt is the loneliness. Remember, too, the lives of the survivors now become more complicated. Some of the tasks performed by the deceased are now assumed by the survivors. The breakdown of the nuclear family—relatives scattered throughout the country—makes the loneliness and these new responsibilities even more poignant.

I have written this book because I want you to know how a deceased's assets are transferred after death, so that *you can control this aspect of death* by making things less complicated for your executor and other survivors.

Sample Situations

There are many cases of inheritances being squandered by the recipients. Bad investments, reckless spending, succumbing to the wiles of the con artist—these things can happen. One reason for these unfortunate occurrences is that perhaps the recipient of the windfall legacy *feels that it is undeserved.* Possibly this is an aspect of *guilt.* Whatever the reasons, there are many cases of money virtually being thrown away. Another reason for a squandered legacy is that the recipient has neither the *prior experience of handling money* nor the development of an *attitude about money.*

One way to avoid these unfortunate occurrences is for the testator to consider using a testamentary trust, which empowers a trustee to supervise the recipient's legacy thus preventing the legacy from being squandered.

But here is another way to avoid the tragedy of the squandered inheritance, and it avoids the costs of a trustee. The legatee should invest the inheritance in the safest investment—perhaps a money market account, a certificate of deposit, or a United States Treasury security. Then wait about a year before buying any big-ticket items, before undertaking any innovative investments, before spending even a penny of the legacy. However, your legatee may not be this prudent, so do give some thought to a testamentary trust.

Money-Saving Suggestion

Make only the most necessary decisions after a loved one's death. Seek the counsel of others but *be careful in your choice of a strong shoulder.*

Part Three

Taxation

16

Introduction

People die, but state and federal governments live on. Death does not abate their appetites for taxes; their fat budgets need constant feeding. The personal representative of an estate has quite a few tax returns to file and taxes to pay. This is the subject we will now tackle. It is the most difficult part of the book, *but you can handle it.* You will soon find out that taxation is not nearly as intriguing a subject as either your will or the administration of an estate.

The discussions on *income taxation of the estate, progressive tax rates, the decedent's final income tax return, a tax audit, and stepped-up basis at time of death* apply to the average person. But keep in mind that at least some of the discussion in this part of the book applies only to estates with substantial assets—about three percent of all estates. However, also keep in mind that many older people are wealthier than they might realize, due to appreciation in the value of their homes, the value of pension benefits, legacies received from other people's estates, investments that have grown, and so on. So look at your *asset inventory.* You might discover that all of Part Three is of great significance to you. Whether all or part of this section of the book applies to you, the material is included in order to offer you a *general overview* of wills, estate administration, and estate taxation.

OVERVIEW OF TAXATION

An estate has quite a few tax returns to file. Here is a summary of these returns, which we will look at more closely in the following chapters.

The *federal individual income tax return* (Form 1040) has to be filed for the person's year of death. If the person has died before April 15th, and the previous year's return has not been filed, then this return also has to be filed. Similarly, if the deceased's state has a state income tax, the *state individual income tax return* for the year of death has to be filed, and perhaps the state income tax return for the previous year also has to be filed.

Any other previous years' *federal individual income tax returns that have not yet been filed* must now be submitted. Also, any *federal individual income tax returns under audit* (or that may soon come under audit) may result in the assessment of an additional federal individual income tax. Similarly, any other previous years' *state individual income tax returns that have not yet been filed,* should now be filed. Also, any *state individual income tax returns under audit* (or that may soon come under audit) may result in the assessment of an additional state individual income tax.

A *federal estate income tax return* (Form 1041) has to be filed by the estate, to report the *income* generated *by the estate* during its administration. Similarly, a *state estate income tax return* must be filed, to report the *income* generated *by the estate* during its administration. The latter, of course, is required only if the deceased's state has an income tax.

A *federal estate tax return* (Form 706) might have to be filed. The tax paid is not an income tax; it is a tax on the *estate assets.* You will learn that the taxable estate of the deceased must exceed $600,000 before this tax is triggered. A *state estate tax return* might have to be filed, and you will learn that, unlike the federal government, some states impose an estate tax on relatively small estates.

Finally, in some states a *state inheritance tax* is owed by *recipients* of estate assets, but closest relatives of the deceased are often exempt from this inheritance tax.

Sample Situation

Tax law is a balancing act between *simplicity* and *fairness.* The simpler tax law is usually the less fair law. An example of a *simple tax law that is not fair* is this hypothetical law of one sentence: "Everyone must pay $8,000 tax per year." Quite simple.

The reverse is also true: the *more complex tax law is usually the fairer law*. The example I have chosen of a complex tax law is not hypothetical. It is an income tax law with which you might have some familiarity: *the tax treatment of Social Security benefits*.

If a Social Security recipient has more than $25,000 of income (or more than $32,000 of income if married and filing jointly), then a portion of social security is subject to income tax. Simple so far. But here the computation headaches begin: To determine whether this $25,000 (or $32,000) threshold amount is exceeded, even tax-exempt income is included (and also *one-half* the social security amount is included); but only *one-half* of the amount by which the $25,000 (or $32,000) is exceeded is taxed; and this amount that is taxed cannot exceed *one-half* the social security benefit, etc. Is this law *fair?* Who knows; fairness is so hard to define. Is it *complex?* Millions of older Americans know the answer. Is it *confusing?* Yes! As if this weren't enough of a problem, these rules are changed for tax years beginning after December 1, 1993, at which time the richest retirees will have 85 percent of Social Security benefits received subject to tax.

So that I do not add to the confusion, I want to distinguish this tax treatment of Social Security benefits from another important question: How much are you permitted to earn without having to *forfeit receiving some of your Social Security?* The answer to this question is neither complex nor confusing. But the answer changes each year.

Money-Saving Suggestion

There are many cases of wealthy people who do not worry about estate tax. After all, the person will be dead when it is time for the estate to pay the tax. *I suggest, however, that you learn how tax dollars can be saved, both income tax dollars and estate tax dollars.* After all, taxation is not a voluntary contribution; the government forces you to pay. A practical attitude is to *balance the amount of tax that legal strategies can avoid with the degree of inconvenience these tax strategies impose.* Keep in mind that an evaluation of tax risks inherent in your personal situation *requires the assistance of a skilled tax consultant.*

17

Estate Taxation

THE TAXABLE ESTATE

The answer to the question "What comprises a taxable estate?" is found in the Internal Revenue Code. The relevant provisions in the code are summarized by this all-encompassing statement: *everything owned by the deceased* is included in the taxable estate.

Form 706, which is the federal estate tax return form, is currently divided into nine sections. It groups your assets as follows:

Schedule A—Real Estate
Schedule B—Stocks and Bonds
Schedule C—Mortgages, Notes, and Cash
Schedule D—Insurance on the Decedent's Life
Schedule E—Jointly Owned Property
Schedule F—Other Miscellaneous Property
Schedule G—Transfers During the Deceased's Life
Schedule H—Powers of Appointment
Schedule I—Annuities

The value of the deceased's estate is the total value of the person's property *at the time of death.* But there is a choice available to the personal representative of the estate; he has the option to value all the assets either as of the date of death or, if lower, as of the date *six months after death.* The rules on this so-called alternate valuation choice are beyond the scope

150

of this volume, but do be aware of the choice. If you have questions, ask your attorney.

From the total value of the deceased's assets certain deductions are made, including: the *administration expenses,* the value of *what is left to a spouse,* and the value of *what is left to a charity.*

The total value of the deceased's assets (valued at the time of death or at the alternate valuation date six months from the date of death), minus allowable deductions, results in the value of the *taxable estate.* The next chapter will outline how much tax is paid on this taxable estate, *payment of which is due nine months after the date of death.*

Notice that the taxable estate includes jointly owned property, which is listed in Schedule E of the tax form. *Many people incorrectly assume that if they put someone else's name on the bankbook, the estate saves taxes.* But, as we have already learned, a joint account *does not reduce the estate tax.* What happens is that the *other person on the account receives the account,* the *will has no effect* on this account, and *probate costs are reduced.*

Sample Situations

Some years ago, a judge with the interesting name of Learned Hand wrote these often-quoted words in his decision on a tax case:

> Over and over again the courts have said that there is nothing sinister in so arranging one's affairs as to keep taxes as low as possible. Everyone does so, rich or poor: and all do right, for nobody owes any public duty to pay more tax than the law demands. *Taxes are enforced exactions, not voluntary contributions.*

Keep in mind the distinctions between *tax avoidance, tax deferral,* and *tax evasion.* There is nothing wrong with avoidance or deferral (it is at least one reason you picked up this book); but tax evasion is a crime. Here are some examples of *avoidance, deferral,* and *evasion;* I have chosen income tax examples with which you might already be familiar: (1) investing in municipal bonds that yield tax exempt interest income is *tax avoidance* (which means you have *legally avoided* the payment of an income tax); (2) investing in an aptly named tax-deferred annuity, where tax on the interest income is not taxed until money is withdrawn, is *tax deferral* (which means a *legally permissible delay* in paying the tax); (3) investing in a money market account at your local bank and not disclosing the taxable income is *tax evasion* because the tax law requires it to be reported and this act of nonreporting, an attempt to escape this law, is the crime of tax evasion.

Money-Saving Suggestion

Find out what tax will be levied on your eventual estate; then seek suggestions from an expert on how to plan your affairs so that this tax can be lessened. Two major areas of tax planning are *gift-giving* and the *maximum use of the marital deduction.* Both of these ideas will be discussed shortly.

Personal representatives can save their respective estates money by seeing that an accurate appraisal report has been made on assets such as real estate and jewelry as soon after death as possible. If there is an audit, it is absolutely necessary to have your valuation expert defend the appraisal value of the property in question. This is the only way to rebut an exorbitant appraisal by the government.

FEDERAL ESTATE TAX

What is the fare paid to the federal government for your final journey? It could be an expensive departure, but one due only from the estates of the rich. If the deceased's net worth is less than $600,000, no federal estate tax is due. In addition to this figure, any amount left to a spouse is free of any federal estate tax. (Keep in mind that the surviving spouse must be a United States citizen.) For example, a married person can leave an estate of $2 million, free of any estate tax, simply by leaving the spouse $1,400,000, and a child $600,000. After all this good news, what is the bad news, you ask? It comes in the form of the *estate tax rate.* For those estates that do owe an estate tax, the rate will be at least a hefty *37 percent.*

Here are some estate tax concepts that may be relevant to your situation; your advisor can discuss them further with you. The estate might be allowed to pay the tax in *installments* over a period of fifteen years. Also, if property in the deceased's estate has been (or will be) *taxed in someone else's estate* within the recent past (or very near future), there is a reduction in the estate tax. (For example, John dies and leaves his estate to Mary; an estate tax is paid; then Mary dies three years later.) If a substantial amount is left to someone who is more than one generation younger than the deceased (for example, a grandfather leaves a legacy to a grandchild), there may be a separate tax called a *generation-skipping tax.*

The personal representatives of estates *should not attempt to complete the federal estate tax return (Form 706)*. Unlike an individual income tax return (the standard Form 1040), which the uninitiated may be able to complete, only experts should grapple with the federal estate tax form. Not only can it be tricky, but a lot of money could be at stake. Once the estate tax form has been completed, be sure that *timely payment* is made to avoid interest and/or penalties to the Internal Revenue Service. In order to prove that payment and filing have been made, send the check and the tax return by *certified mail* with a *return receipt requested.*

Sample Situations

Many estates have not been planned for the purpose of saving estate tax dollars. The federal estate tax could have been reduced if only certain changes in asset ownership had been implemented. In those cases where federal taxes are avoided, two techniques frequently appear: *testamentary trusts and gifting assets.* The former saves estate tax in the estate of the beneficiary of the trust. An example of a testamentary trust is presented in the money-saving suggestion that follows. The latter technique of gifting is described in the next section.

Money-Saving Suggestion

Let us take the situation of two sisters, Joan and Mary. Each has a net worth of $600,000, and their one relative is nephew Paul. Joan wants to leave everything to Mary; Mary wants to leave everything to Joan. When they are both gone, Paul is to receive their fortunes.

I suggest that Joan leave her estate in a testamentary trust, from which Mary can draw income annually. Upon Mary's later death, Mary's assets, and the principal of the testamentary trust established in Joan's will, are distributed to Paul.

As for Mary's will, it can be a mirror-image of Joan's. If Mary dies first, then Joan receives the income from the testamentary trust in Mary's will. Upon Joan's later death, Joan's assets, and the principal of the trust established in Mary's will, are distributed to Paul.

No federal estate tax is paid by either estate. However, if the first to die had left the $600,000 outright to her sister (rather than to a testamentary trust for the benefit of her sister), *when the survivor dies there is a taxable estate of $1,200,000, with a tax that could be as high as $240,000.* However, with my testamentary trust suggestion, the *survivor* of the two sisters leaves a $600,000 taxable estate, because the "other" $600,000—*the money left in a trust by the first sister to die*—is not taxed in the surviving sister's estate. For wealthy readers, this suggestion can save your estate a *bundle*.

GIFT TAX

The federal government has (and a few states, including New York, have) a gift tax so that people cannot escape the estate tax by giving away their money, stock, or real estate, etc., thus dying without any estate (or with an estate that has been substantially reduced). *A gift tax is a tax paid by a person who gives a large gift.* It is a tax that supplements the estate tax. People who receive the large gifts do not pay any tax on the amount of these gifts. The person making the gift reports this transfer of assets on IRS Form 709. In general, this form must be filed by April 15th after the calendar year in which the gift was made.

How large is a "large gift"? For the federal government, large means over $10,000. So, if you give your nephew a $9,000 gift, there is no worry about taxes for you or him—no estate tax, no gift tax, and no income tax. *Gifts of amounts up to $10,000 to each recipient during a calendar year, to as many people to whom you want to make a gift, year after year, are not subject to a gift tax.* This $10,000 limitation is called the *annual exclusion amount,* that is, the maximum amount that can be given annually to any number of recipients without any worry of gift taxes. (Some of you might remember when this amount was $3,000.)

If a gift of money is given, it is easy to determine how much $10,000 is. But suppose stock that cost $5,000 is given as a gift when it is worth $10,000? This is a $10,000 gift—the value at the time the gift is made.

In the last section, we learned that an individual can leave $600,000 without the estate being taxed by the federal government. Let me expand a bit on this. Since the gift tax is supplementary to an estate tax, the $600,000 amount is the *total untaxed amount that either can be given away as a gift during your life or left in your estate.* Therefore, you can give a gift of a few hundred thousand dollars during your lifetime and not have to pay any federal gift tax. At the time of death, however, the amount *free of federal estate tax* is reduced by the total amount of your taxable gifts. Perhaps the following example will help to explain this law:

John gave his son $210,000 in 1984. John dies in 1990 leaving an estate of $500,000. *There is a federal estate tax on $100,000, and the amount of tax is $37,000.* Why? Because $10,000 of the $210,000 gift does not enter into the computation (recall the $10,000 annual exclusion); the $200,000 portion of the gift plus the $500,000 estate equal $700,000; but only a total of $600,000 of gifts and estate is free of tax; this leaves $100,000 upon which a tax is levied; the federal estate tax on this amount is currently $37,000 (37 percent of the taxable $100,000).

A final point: If a husband and wife *join* in giving a gift, a gift of up to $20,000 per year can be given to each recipient, and repeated year after year. It can be given to as many people each year to whom this couple wishes to make a gift, and there are no gift tax consequences. The $600,000 amount is not reduced. The reason a husband and wife can jointly give up to $20,000 is because each can be considered the giver of one-half, or $10,000, which is the amount of the *annual exclusion* discussed earlier.

Sample Situation

Telling a wealthy person to give away money to save estate taxes is like telling an incorrigible ninety-three-year-old to stop smoking cigars, to abstain from drinking, and to cease carousing. It is a justifiable attitude for the elder person to conclude that the estate tax—like cigars, liquor, and carousing—does not have any adverse personal effect. *It is the estate that pays the tax.* This attitude has been expressed by many people, and there is nothing wrong with it. I have presented options so that you can make an informed decision. *What is right for you should not be questioned or judged by anyone.*

Money-Saving Suggestion

A wealthy individual is advised to consider giving property worth $10,000 each year to many people, year after year, to reduce the eventual estate tax. The estate will have a substantially reduced estate tax, although it means that the benefactor has deprived himself of the enjoyment of the gift property by having given it away.

Let us review the tax consequences when a mother gifts $10,000 to her child:

Mother does not pay any federal gift tax on this gift, because it does not exceed $10,000. The child pays neither a federal gift tax nor a federal income tax on this gift. When Mother dies, the government has lost the opportunity to impose an estate tax on the $10,000. Additionally, the government has lost the opportunity to impose an estate tax on *the amount by which the $10,000 might have appreciated from the time of the gift to the time of the mother's death.* For example, if she had not made the gift and then lived many more years, the $10,000 amount could be worth much more at the time of her death.

The $10,000 gift does not appear on the mother's individual income tax return. *But future income tax might be saved,* because the tax on the annual interest from this $10,000 gift will be paid by the child, who possibly is taxed at a lower tax rate than the wealthier mother. This idea requires us to take a look at *progressive tax rates.* Let us do so.

PROGRESSIVE TAX RATES

A *progressive tax rate* increases as the amount to be taxed increases. But the increased tax rate affects only the *additional dollars.* For example, let us look at the progressive estate tax rates imposed on taxable estates over $600,000. The tax on an estate valued between *$600,000 and $750,000* is 37 percent of the amount over $600,000. The tax on an estate valued between *$600,000 and $1,000,000* is also *37 percent* of the amount between $600,000 and $750,000, *plus* a tax of *39 percent* on the amount between $750,000 and $1,000,000. This *progression of increasing rates* continues until the maximum rate, which has been as high as 55 percent, is reached. (The 55 percent has been applied to the portion of an estate that exceeds $3,000,000.) Keep in mind that these rates may change from time to time, through amendment of federal tax laws by Congress.

Sample Situation

Here is a situation that demonstrates how *progressive tax rates* affect not only estate tax planning, but also *income tax planning:*

Facts: John is married and files a joint income tax return. His total taxable income for the year will be $50,000. He has $100,000 to invest. His bank is offering a certificate of deposit *yielding 7 percent taxable interest income.* His alternative investment is a municipal bond *yielding 6 percent tax exempt interest income.* Assume that John's tax bracket, the percentage of tax on his highest taxed dollar, is *28 percent* (keeping in mind that this tax bracket can vary from year to year, depending both on *John's income* and the *tax rates* for that year).

Question: Which investment will yield the greater "after tax" amount, the investment yielding the *7 percent taxable interest income* or the investment yielding *the 6 percent tax exempt interest income?*

Answer: The 6 percent tax exempt investment will put $6,000 in his pocket, as compared to the *after tax* amount of only $5,040 from the 7 percent taxable investment.

Explanation: The $7,000 yield from the 7 percent taxable investment will have a tax of $1,960 (28 percent of $7,000). Therefore, the $7,000 taxable yield will net John $5,040 after the federal tax is paid ($960 less than the income from the tax exempt investment).

Conclusion: John should consider purchasing the tax exempt investment.

Money-Saving Suggestion

Tax planning is important for wealthy individuals, because their potential tax—both estate tax and income tax—can be a substantial amount. Remember once again what you have learned throughout this book about the need for an asset *inventory;* sometimes people do not realize that with the passage of time their assets have grown just like inflation has grown. A person, although surely not wealthy, may have a home that has quite dramatically appreciated in value. Remember, too, that everything you own at the time of death is included in your gross estate, including all your bankbooks (even those that list your favorite niece as a joint owner or as the "in trust for" beneficiary).

As for the federal estate tax, someone with a net worth of under $600,000 would probably have only minimum benefit from estate tax planning. But the estate of someone with assets of over $600,000 will save (under current law) at least thirty-seven cents for each dollar that is removed from the eventual taxable estate. This amount of potential savings increases as the value of the estate increases, due to the progressive tax rates. The eventual estate of a multi-millionaire can *save a fortune through estate tax planning.*

STATE DEATH TAXES

State death taxes are of two varieties: an *inheritance tax* and a *state estate tax.*

About fifteen states have an inheritance tax. This tax is imposed upon *those who receive the deceased's assets.* Fortunately, surviving spouses, children, and grandchildren are either totally or partially exempt from this inheritance tax in most of these states. However, other individuals (often including brothers and sisters of the deceased) who inherit the deceased's assets have to pay the inheritance tax in those fifteen or so states that levy it. A state where this tax is particularly severe is Iowa.

Every state has a *state estate tax* (now that Nevada has adopted it). There are three ideas about a state estate tax that might be of interest to you: (1) Some states impose this tax even on relatively *small estates* (for example, an estate of $100,000); however, the tax is *much lower* than the federal estate tax (for example, the tax might be 5 percent of the estate value). (2) Various states only impose this tax on large estates— those valued at more than $600,000. (3) In some of the states that only impose the tax on large estates, the state estate tax is eliminated by the *federal estate tax credit* for all or a portion of any state estate tax paid by the estate.

A *tax credit* reduces *a tax* by the amount of the credit. This can be contrasted to a tax deduction, which reduces *the amount which is taxable.* For example, a tax credit of one dollar reduces a tax by one dollar; a tax deduction of one dollar is less valuable, because it only *saves what would have been the tax* on that one dollar.

Returning now to the federal estate tax credit for state estate taxes, there is a *limit on how much of a state death tax* (whether an inheritance tax or an estate tax) is allowed as a federal estate tax credit. This limit depends on the total value of the estate, and is stated in an Internal Revenue Service chart (see Appendix B). For example, if an estate is valued at $1,100,000, the amount of the state death tax paid—up to a maximum amount of $38,800 (the Internal Revenue Service chart gives me this amount)—is the amount allowed as a federal estate tax credit. From this flows the following two examples: First, if the state death tax on a $1,100,000 estate is $20,000, then the federal estate tax credit (or reduction) is $20,000 and, therefore, the federal government has indirectly paid the estate's state death tax. Second, if the state death tax on a $1,100,000 estate is $40,000, then the federal estate tax credit (or reduction) is *limited to* $38,800 (the amount in the IRS chart for estates of $1,100,000).

If the federal tax credit for state death tax paid is still a bit confusing, talk to your attorney or tax consultant. What is within your control is your ability to establish which state is your state of domicile. *You do not want two states fighting over who receives the state death tax.*

Sample Situations

Suppose John is a resident of a state that has an inheritance tax that is paid by *someone* (other than a spouse, children, and grandchildren) *receiving assets from the estate.* It also has an *estate tax* that taxes only estates of substantial value. John leaves his son $125,000 and his brother $30,000. John's estate *pays no federal or state estate tax;* his brother *pays an inheritance tax;* his son *does not pay an inheritance tax.*

Here is another sample situation: John is a resident of New York State, a state that has *no inheritance tax* but does have *an estate tax* (on an estate where a nonspouse receives over $108,343). Again, his son and brother are left $125,000 and $30,000 respectively. The *estate pays an estate tax of about $2,750;* the *son and brother pay no inheritance tax;* there is *no federal tax owed because the estate is less than $600,000.*

Money-Saving Suggestion

If an estate incurs a federal tax, there is a reduction of the federal estate tax by the tax credit for the state death tax. However, the estate might *not* be allowed a federal estate tax credit that equals the *entire amount of the state death tax,* because the credit is subject to the limits outlined in the IRS chart in Appendix B.

WHEN A SPOUSE INHERITS

If you are *married,* then this section is an important one for you. I will repeat the great news for married couples. *Everything you inherit from your spouse is free of any federal estate tax. Any gift you receive from your spouse is also free of any federal gift tax.* (Again, remember that the surviving spouse—the one who receives the inheritance or gift—is assumed to be a United States citizen.)

There is a big problem, however, despite the tax-free treatment of assets inherited by a spouse. *What happens when the surviving spouse dies?* Quite likely, the estate of the surviving spouse will contain all or a considerable portion of the assets of both husband and wife, resulting in quite a significant tax being levied upon the estate.

Here is an example: Mr. Smith is worth $600,000, and Mrs. Smith also is worth $600,000. There is no estate tax when the first spouse dies. But there will be a huge estate tax (perhaps as high as $240,000) when the remaining spouse dies, *because his or her estate will probably be in excess of $1.2 million.*

Earlier I demonstrated how two sisters, each worth $600,000, could avoid estate tax (and the surviving sister, in addition to her own $600,000, has the use of the deceased sister's $600,000). Similarly, a married couple can avoid an estate tax on a combined estate of $1.2 million. Like the two sisters, Mr. and Mrs. Smith can use a testamentary trust. My next money-saving suggestion shows how a married couple can avoid estate tax on a combined estate of $1,200,000.

Sample Situation

Married couples like to use a testamentary trust to be sure that legacies to the children are protected in the event that the *surviving spouse re-marries.* For some people the tax savings motive is secondary. The following money-saving suggestion explains the twofold purpose of this $600,000 trust: *to assure that the children of the marriage receive a legacy and to save taxes when the widow or widower dies.*

Money-Saving Suggestions

A testamentary trust can have dramatic estate tax savings. *Also, this trust clearly specifies the ultimate recipient of the money.* Mr. and Mrs. Smith, each worth $600,000, can leave a total amount of $1,200,000 without any estate tax in *either* estate. Each will simply states: "I leave $600,000 to my trustee, the XYZ Trust Company, for the benefit of the following people. My trustee is to distribute all the income to my spouse annually. Upon my spouse's death the principal is to be distributed evenly among our three children, and this trust is to terminate."

The $600,000 that the spouse leaves in trust (for the benefit of the *surviving spouse and then for the children*) is not taxable, because $600,000 can be left to anyone free of any estate tax. Therefore, the estate of the first deceased spouse pays no estate tax. This amount held in trust is then free of tax in the surviving spouse's estate, since it is not considered to be the surviving spouse's property (even though the surviving spouse had substantial use of these funds). In addition, the surviving spouse can then leave the children another $600,000, also free of any estate tax. The children (or any other legatees) of Mr. and Mrs. Smith can thereby receive $1.2 million undiminished by any federal estate tax.

Suppose a spouse has more than $600,000 and has these three objectives: (1) leaving this additional amount to his *spouse;* (2) using a trust, so as to be able to determine the *ultimate recipient(s)* after the surviving spouse's death; and (3) having this bequest *qualify for the marital deduction.* Can these three objectives be realized? Yes, through the use of what is called a QTIP (Qualified Terminable Interest Property) Trust. These trusts obviously are relevant only to the very wealthiest of couples, but I did want to at least mention the QTIP Trust before moving on to a topic relevant to every estate—the *deceased's final income tax return.*

18

Income Taxation

THE FINAL INCOME TAX RETURN

The deceased's final income tax return is filed by the personal representative of the estate. It is the same Form 1040 that would have been filed had the person lived. There are a few decisions that have to be made by the personal representative, including: the choice of *filing status* if the deceased was married, the tax treatment of *medical expenses,* and the tax treatment of income from *United States Savings Bonds.*

A *joint tax return* can be filed for the year of death if there is a surviving spouse. I suggest that three returns be tentatively prepared: one for the *deceased spouse alone,* using the married-filing-separately status; one for the surviving spouse alone, also using the married-filing-separately status; and one for *both husband and wife,* using the married-filing-jointly status. Readers and their tax consultant will have to determine the less costly choice (either *filing jointly* or *married-filing-separately*).

The *cost of medical care* provided to the deceased (paid within a year after death) may be taken as a deduction *either* on the deceased's final year's *federal individual income tax return or* on the *federal estate tax return* (but not on both). Many times there is no tax savings realized, *regardless of which of these two options is chosen.* If the unreimbursed portion of the medical expenses is less than 7.5 percent of your adjusted gross income, it is disregarded on an individual's income tax return. If there is no estate tax owed, the medical expense deduction taken on an estate tax return is meaningless. The choice becomes important when *only* the income tax *or* the estate tax can be reduced by deducting the medical expenses. Make sure you take it *on the one where tax is reduced.* The choice is also important when *both* the income tax and the estate tax could be reduced by deducting the medical expenses. Make sure you take it *on the one that results in greater tax savings.*

The third decision is the treatment of *United States Savings Bonds* interest, which for many older persons is substantial if it has accrued over a number of years. It can be reported on the *deceased's final income tax return,* on the *estate's income tax return,* or on the *beneficiary's income tax return* (if the bonds are distributed to a beneficiary who sells them). Do some calculating before making your decision.

Sample Situation

Estate executors and/or administrators need to file Form 56 with the Internal Revenue Service. This form is the personal representative's notification to the IRS of his or her appointment to handle the affairs of the deceased. It advises the IRS where to send notices, including any audit notices.

I suggest you file this form. *Otherwise, you are likely to miss an opportunity to question any income tax audit findings of the Internal Revenue Service.* This is because a statute of limitations—the time in which you must challenge the IRS's ruling—could expire *without your even knowing of the existence of an audit.* The statute of limitations begins to run from the time the Internal Revenue Service *mails* a statutory notice to the taxpayer, not when the taxpayer receives it. Keep in mind that the IRS is required to send notices only to the *last known address* of a taxpayer. *The burden is on the personal representative of the estate to let the government know where mail is to be sent.*

Money-Saving Suggestions

In addition to the deceased's final income tax return, there may also be the necessity of filing the deceased's previous year's income tax return. This occurs when a deceased has died early in the year (before April 15th), before having filed it.

In such cases, the personal representative of the estate should take advantage of the *four-month automatic extension of time to file the previous year's tax return by filing Form 4868.* It is this previous year's tax return that sometimes presents some difficulties in fact gathering. This is particularly true when death occurs in late March or early April, close to the filing deadline. If matters are in a turmoil, it is advisable to obtain this extension so that an accurate tax return can then be prepared. Realize that what you are obtaining is an extension of time to *file* the tax return, not an extension of time to *pay* the tax that might be due. Therefore, estimate the amount owed and mail a check for this amount along with Form 4868. Remember to put the deceased's social security number on the check.

In addition to this automatic four-month extension, a further extension can be requested by filing Form 2688. Although this further extension is not automatically granted, a reason such as the death of the taxpayer or incomplete records is usually sufficient for the IRS to grant this additional extension of time to file. I do not recommend seeking this additional extension. Why delay matters so long?

INCOME TAXATION OF AN ESTATE

An estate generates income during the time it is administered, and thus *an estate might have to pay an income tax just like a person would.* Here are two examples of how an estate generates income during its administration: stocks owned by the deceased pay dividend income; bank accounts owned by the deceased generate interest income. The estate income tax return is Form 1041, similar to the individual income tax return (the Form 1040).

The estate income tax return must give the estate's identification number. (As soon as the executor is appointed, he files Form SS-4 with the Internal Revenue Service to obtain this identification number.) The income received by the estate is listed, the allowable deductions are subtracted from the income, the tax is computed, and the return is signed and filed by the personal representative of the estate.

In addition to reading the instructions carefully, here are a few tips: (1) decide whether to elect a calendar year or a fiscal year; (2) funeral expenses are not deductible on the estate's income tax return (but remember to deduct these expenses on the estate tax return); (3) administration expenses (such as executor's commission and attorney's fee) can be taken *either* on the *estate's income tax return* or on the *estate tax return;* (4) distributions from the estate (generally up to the amount of the income) to beneficiaries are deductions on the estate's income tax return.

The estate income tax return is more complex than your individual income tax return. However, if you can do your own taxes, *you can possi-*

bly do an estate income tax return. Realize that you might be adept at doing your own income tax return only because you have been *doing it for years;* the Form 1041 is a *new experience for the executor.*

Taxes might be saved if the assets of an estate are distributed slowly. This is because the income tax on the yield from these assets may be less if this yield is taxable on the estate income tax return rather than taxable on the recipient's income tax return. The following sample situation demonstrates how slowness is sometimes tax-wise.

Sample Situation

John is a successful salesman and his taxable income is about $100,000 each year. His elderly aunt dies and John is her only legatee (he is the residuary legatee). John is to receive the only asset she owned, a $50,000 certificate of deposit yielding 10 percent interest income annually ($5,000 each year). If there is a delay in distributing the legacy, the $5,000 interest income is taxable to the estate (and is taxed at the rate applicable for $0 to $5,000 of income). This happens because the estate has not made a distribution to John and, therefore, the estate has not received an income distribution deduction. The estate (which earned the income) pays a *lower estate income tax* on this yield than John, who might be in a *higher income tax bracket* (quite likely, since in this sample situation John has taxable income of $100,000, so the additional $5,000 of taxable income would be taxed at the rate applicable for $100,000 to $105,000 of income). But *be reasonable in how long you delay distribution.*

Money-Saving Suggestion

Here is a suggestion (and a warning) to personal representatives of estates. You could be *personally liable* for taxes owed and unpaid by an estate—the income taxes (the tax computed on the federal individual income tax Form 1040 and the federal estate income tax Form 1041) and the estate taxes (the tax computed on the federal estate tax Form 706). This would occur if the personal representative of the estate distributes all the estate's assets before paying all these taxes. Then the government could reach into the pocket of the personal representative (executor or administrator).

In addition to the possibility of personal liability if all taxes are not paid, a raft of letters will be forthcoming from the Internal Revenue Service, your state tax people, and the legatees. To sort it all out a few years later is an expensive and frustrating exercise. The timely filing of all tax returns and the payment of all the taxes that are due are essential responsibilities, but be sure that the estate is not paying more than necessary to the government. What happens if too little is paid to the government? Let us take a look at a tax audit.

TAX AUDIT

A tax audit is not the terrifying experience one so often imagines. Personal representatives of estates should stay calm if an audit is announced. The auditor *requests* information; you *provide* the information; the auditor *decides* whether the tax return accurately computes the tax owed; the auditor may *assess* an additional tax on the estate; if the assessment is correct, an additional tax is *paid.*

If you are *worried* about the audit, then go to the audit with an attorney, an accountant, or a person qualified by written examination to represent taxpayers before the Internal Revenue Service. If you are *terrified* about the audit, then stay home and put your trust completely in the hands of a competent representative.

But if you follow these suggestions, you will have a worry-free tax life: *report* all the deceased's assets on the *estate tax return,* and all the income from the estate on the *estate income tax return;* on these returns *deduct only* those expenses that were incurred and are allowable as deductions; *be assertive,* however, and even when in doubt do not be intimidated by the auditor.

Suppose you disagree with the auditor's decision. You have a right to appeal within the Internal Revenue Service itself. After that appeal, your ultimate relief is to take one of two approaches: either pay the additional tax and then institute a lawsuit for a refund in the Federal District Court (or the Federal Court of Claims); or, alternatively (and the more practical approach), do not pay the additional tax and immediately start a lawsuit in the United States Tax Court. Be aware of the statute of limitations (the time in which a lawsuit must be commenced) for a lawsuit begun in the United States Tax Court. It must commence within *ninety days* from the date on the *notice of deficiency* that candidly advises you that *you have ninety days to petition the United States Tax Court.* The lawsuit is started by the taxpayer, who files a legal document, called a petition, with the United States Tax Court.

Sample Situation

Experience teaches that *the less said at an audit the better the results.* It is better to let your records speak for themselves whenever possible, so be sure to keep accurate and complete records.

Here are some of the items that are frequently requested at the audit of an estate tax return: (1) the deceased's Form 1040 individual income tax returns for the past three years, (2) all Form 1041 estate income tax returns, (3) bank and brokerage statements for the three years prior to death and the entire period of the estate administration, (4) all life insurance policies, (5) any personal property insurance policy, (6) proof of payment of all items deducted on any tax return, (7) the estate checkbook and all the cancelled checks, (8) any gift tax returns, and (9) appraisals of the value of estate assets.

Money-Saving Suggestions

The most important advice I can give is *not to be intimidated* by a tax auditor. Keep in mind these eight suggestions on audit etiquette: *arrive* on time; *bring* the requested information; *listen* carefully; *do not apologize; do not insult the auditor* (it never helps and sometimes hurts); *do not dump* boxes of receipts on the auditor's desk; *do not sign* anything (go home and calmly review the auditor's findings); *do not say* a final nasty remark (the auditor is a taxpayer, too). GOOD LUCK!

Finally, try to make the auditor's job easy by providing requested information promptly. The reason this approach achieves more favorable results is that the auditor has spent less time on the audit than had been anticipated. He need not justify (to himself or his supervisor) the long hours of tedious work *by deciding every questionable issue in favor of the government.*

STEPPED-UP BASIS AT TIME OF DEATH

If you sell real estate, a share of stock, or any other asset at a gain, you are required to pay *income tax on the amount of the taxable gain.* Your *taxable gain* is the amount by which your *selling price* exceeds your *basis;* your *taxable loss* is the amount by which your basis exceeds your selling price. In most situations, *basis* is a tax term that means your *cost, plus* the cost of any *improvements, less* any *tax depreciation.*

With this knowledge, let us now compute the taxable gain on the sale of a plot of land. If you paid $100,000 for the land, spent an additional $10,000 to have the land cleared, and then sold the land for $200,000, *your gain is $90,000.* This is because the *selling price* of $200,000 *exceeds* the *basis* of $110,000 (which is the $100,000 purchase price plus the $10,000 cost of the clearing) *by $90,000.*

But special tax treatment is given to assets received from a decedent's estate (except for appreciated property acquired by gift within one year of the decedent's death). The recipient of the asset receives a basis that is called a *stepped-up basis at the time of death.* This description is appropriate, since the basis (the amount *above which* is the taxable gain) is stepped-up (or increased) to the *value at death.*

The following example, using the same numbers found in the previous illustration, shows the *tax benefit of a stepped-up basis at the time of death:*

John buys a plot of land for $100,000. He has the land cleared for $10,000. Years later he dies and leaves the house to his nephew. The value of the house at John's death is $200,000. The nephew's gain on his ultimate sale of the land is *measured from $200,000* and not from his uncle's $110,000 basis. The nephew has received what tax people call stepped-up basis at time of death. *The $90,000 appreciation during the uncle's ownership is never taxed.*

This is a significant tax benefit for families who own property that has appreciated in value. *Income tax is never paid on the appreciation in value of such property for the period between the time the property was acquired and the owner's death.*

Keep in mind that if property has *declined* in value prior to death, the basis for the person inheriting the property is also the date of death value, which is called a *stepped-down* basis. For example, if you inherited Grandmother's stock, which cost her $60 a share but is only worth $55 per share at the time of her death, your stepped-down basis—used to measure your eventual gain or loss upon sale—is $55.

Sample Situation

If a more well-off taxpayer gives gifts to members of the family, perhaps this taxpayer should give *money rather than stock that has appreciated in value.* Here is a case that helps to explain why:

Father, a widower, has $400,000 in money market accounts. He also has $400,000 worth of stock that years ago only cost him $200,000. Father is giving gifts to his child. Should he give money or stocks? Money. Why?

If he owns the stock until he dies, and his child (or anyone else) then inherits the stock, neither the father nor the child will pay an income tax on any growth from the time the father *bought it until his death*. Why? When the stock is sold by the heir, the gain is measured from the *stepped-up basis at the time of the father's death*.

However, if Father *gives* the stock (rather than willing it), when the child sells the stock, *the gain is measured from the cost at which the father bought it.*

Money-Saving Suggestions

If you possess property that has increased substantially in value (real estate, stock, etc.), *I suggest you do some serious calculating before deciding to sell (or give away) the asset.* If you hold onto it for the rest of your life, your heir can sell the property, and neither you nor your heir incur any income tax on its appreciation in value during the time of your ownership.

The preceding suggestion is unrealistic if you definitely want to sell the property, and particularly unrealistic if you have *a need for the cash proceeds.* Like any suggestion that saves tax dollars, what a person wants or needs is equally as important as the tax-wise suggestion. Some people make decisions that are not the best ones strictly from a tax point of view. But if it is what the person wants, despite a favorable tax alternative, then so be it. You decide, but there is nothing wrong in listening to the advice of others.

19

Family Businesses, and Charities

THE FAMILY FARM AND OTHER FAMILY BUSINESSES

The value of real estate owned by the deceased, including the family farm, is included in the gross estate. The fair market value is determined by an appraiser, and is estimated to be what someone might be willing to pay for the property. Generally the appraiser bases the estimate on recent selling prices of similar pieces of property.

But there is a problem. The Internal Revenue Service requires the appraiser to base the estimate on an assumption that the property is put to its *highest and best use*. A farm, for example, located close to a crowded urban center, might be valued, not as a farm, but as a tract of land that could be a potentially attractive location for commercial or residential use. Big trouble for farmers!

There is, however, a relief provision in the Internal Revenue Code, and farms, as well as other real estate, can be exempt from this highest-and-best-use standard. To obtain this relief, there are various specific tests that must be met. Essentially, *if the farm or business real estate is a substantial percentage of the deceased's estate, and has been used for such purposes for a substantial period of time, then the valuation will be exempt from the highest-and-best-use standard.*

The rationale for this tax-relief provision allowing a lower actual (or special use) valuation is quite understandable. The government considers it unfair to place a heavy tax on the family, *because payment of the tax might require the family to sell or mortgage the farm in order to pay the estate tax.*

170

The estate tax is normally paid nine months after death. However, another relief provision to help a *family farm or other business* is the availability of *installment payments.* If a family business is a substantial percentage of the deceased's estate, the taxing authorities might permit payment of the tax to be made over a fifteen-year period. Although there is interest charged on this deferred payment, the interest on at least some of this amount is lower than the prevailing rate of interest charged by a bank.

Both of the above-described situations, *special use valuation* and *installment payment of estate taxes,* need careful planning. Keep in mind that the tax benefit is "recaptured" if there is a change of use or ownership *during a substantial period of time after being inherited.*

Sample Situation

A crucial time for a family-owned business is the death of the family member most active in the business. Make sure someone has been educated in every aspect of running the company. Otherwise, the business might have to be *discontinued;* even worse, legal action might be instituted against the estate for *unfulfilled commitments* made by the deceased owner that no one is now available to complete.

Money-Saving Suggestion

So often have I emphasized the importance of *everyone* keeping an *inventory,* and I hope you remember my advice that you *must tell your executor where this inventory and other important papers are kept.*

Business owners have the additional tasks of *choosing a successor* and *keeping this person* continuously updated on such matters as: accounts payable and receivable, existing contracts, recent amendments to pension plans and other employee benefits, and every other aspect of the business. For those readers who do not want to divulge *everything* to the successor, I suggest that at least you tell the successor where this *confidential information is kept.* Perhaps with the passage of time you will entrust your successor with the actual information. But, in the meantime, make sure all your confidential records are *complete* and your successor knows *where they are kept.*

CHARITABLE TRUSTS

We have already discussed the estate tax benefit of leaving money or other property to a charity (see chapter 7): those dollars (or the value of other property) left to a charity are not subject to an estate tax.

We have also discussed the use of a testamentary trust (see chapter 8), whereby a testator leaves money or other property to a beneficiary, but the money or property is to be controlled by a trustee. The reasons a testator might give for doing this are varied, but could include: a lack of confidence in the beneficiary (thereby appointing someone else to control the assets in the trust) or a desire to determine *who receives the assets after the lifetime beneficiary dies.*

Let us combine these two ideas of leaving money to a charity and using a testamentary trust. The following example of a charitable remainder trust demonstrates how they could be combined and expressed in the will of John's father:

> I bequeath the sum of $400,000 to my trustee, ABC Trust Company, in trust nevertheless, for the benefit of my son, John. *My trustee is to distribute annually seven percent of the net fair market value of the trust assets, as valued annually, to my son, John,* and upon his death my trustee is to distribute the principal to DEF Charity and terminate the trust.

The estate is allowed a deduction for the fair market value of what the charity eventually is to receive. The value of what John will receive (which is referred to as his unitrust interest) depends on the age of John when his father dies. If John is young, the value of the charitable deduction is not so great, because the charity receives the money far in the future. Also, notice the words giving John a fixed percentage of the trust annually. The law requires the charitable trust to distribute annually (out of interest or principal or both) a fixed percent of the trust principal (at least 5 percent) in order for the estate to qualify for a charitable deduction. The higher the percentage to John, the lower the charitable deduction. The law *does not allow an estate tax charitable deduction* if what John receives is measured *only* by the income earned annually, even if upon his death the funds in the trust are to be distributed to a charity.

Sample Situation

Joan is in her mid-eighties. She has a net worth of $800,000. Her only relative is her younger and poorer sister, Matilda. Joan wants to leave her entire estate to Matilda. Joan really does not care who receives what is left of the $800,000 after both she and Matilda are dead. Joan, however, has always had an admiration for the good work done by the New York Foundling Hospital. A *charitable remainder trust* might be the appropriate estate plan for Joan. She can help her sister, help a charity, and save her estate some taxes. She can leave the $800,000 to a trustee for Matilda's benefit; Matilda receives a fixed percentage of this amount each year; and upon Matilda's death, the New York Foundling Hospital receives all the assets held by the trust.

Definitely, the estate tax on Joan's estate will be *lower* as a result of the charitable remainder trust because, in addition to the tax-free $600,000 amount, the charitable deduction at least partially wipes out the remaining $200,000 in the taxable estate. *Definitely,* poorer Matilda's estate will have no estate tax for a reason unrelated to the charity being named by Joan as the ultimate recipient. Matilda's estate is not taxed, because *none* of the $800,000 in the trust will be included in Matilda's taxable estate. Why? Because Matilda did not have the right to name the ultimate recipient, a charity or otherwise, upon her death. This ultimate beneficiary, New York Foundling Hospital, was *already chosen by Joan.*

Money-Saving Suggestion

To those who plan on discussing charitable trusts with their attorney, I suggest you read these descriptions of three types of charitable trusts that currently qualify under federal tax law for the estate tax charitable deduction.

A *charitable remainder annuity trust* is required to pay annually to the lifetime beneficiary a definite percentage of the *value of the assets* (the federal tax law establishes the *minimum* percentage, which is currently at 5 percent), *as valued on the day the trust is established,* which for a testamentary trust would be the date of the testator's death.

A *charitable remainder unitrust* is required to pay annually to the lifetime beneficiary a definite percentage of the *value of the assets* (again, the federal tax law establishes the *minimum* percentage, which is currently at 5 percent), *as valued annually.*

The difference between these trusts is the *time* at which the principal of the trust is *valued.* They are similar in that both require a *minimum percentage of the trust assets* to be distributed annually to the lifetime beneficiary, and the person establishing either trust *chooses the trustee.*

This last aspect distinguishes these two charitable remainder trusts from another type of charitable trust called a *pooled income fund.* With this type of trust, the *charity is the trustee* and the funds are pooled (combined) with funds already contributed by others. The lifetime beneficiary receives a prorated portion of the earnings from the pool of funds.

This brings us to the end of our taxation discussion. We now move on to Part Four to take consider some additional ideas that might be of interest.

Part Four

Final Thoughts

20

Some Additional Ideas

OUR LEGAL SYSTEM

Our legal system has become difficult for the average person to comprehend, and that is why I have tried to explain wills and estate administration in what I hope is an understandable way. But why is the law so complex?

First, our lives are complex and so are the rights and responsibilities we enjoy under the law. Adding to this complexity is the fact that we live under two sets of laws, federal and state. A second reason for the law's complexity is that *we want our rights and responsibilities specifically enumerated.* Therefore, so many legal forms are required for even the simplest of transactions, because people want to be *definite* in their dealings. Third, the law is complex because its goal of *fairness* is reachable only with statutes that try to cover every imaginable situation. This results in laws that are *overprotective,* that might apply to situations where protection is not needed.

From the drawing of a will to the final account prepared by the personal representative of the estate, dozens of documents are written, reviewed, revised, signed, recorded, challenged, and appealed. Time-consuming, yes, but the end result has a dramatic effect on the lives of many people. The best response to this legal bureaucracy is an educated public. If those who are affected by the legal system have a *general understanding of that system,* then the law's complexity will be far less frustrating.

Sample Situation

A woman died and her surviving spouse received all her assets—consisting of real estate, bank accounts, and pension benefits—because they were held in joint ownership with the right of survivorship. An appraisal of the real estate was required. In fact, it was important for the surviving spouse to have this appraisal, and the reason for the appraisal is the subject of this sample situation.

Let us assume that the real estate is valued at $500,000 at the time of the woman's death. Further assume that the real estate originally cost $200,000 some years ago. If there is a valid appraisal showing the $500,000 date-of-death-value, a potential reduction of income tax, upon an eventual sale of this property by the surviving husband, can result. Let me explain.

When a husband and a wife jointly own an asset, the law concludes that one-half is owned by the husband and other half is owned by the wife. The half owned by the now deceased wife receives the stepped-up basis at time of her death, which means that this half has a $250,000 (the value at death) tax basis for measuring gain on the sale. The husband's half has his original basis of one-half of the $200,000 cost, or $100,000. Therefore, if the husband now sells the property for $500,000, the gain on the sale of this property (which only cost $200,000) is $150,000. This $150,000 is the difference between the total basis of $350,000 (the deceased wife's $250,000 stepped-up basis, plus the husband's $100,000 basis) and the selling price of $500,000. Incidentally, of this $150,000, perhaps only $25,000 is taxable; under current law, if the eligibility requirements (including age, ownership, and use) are met, the sale would qualify for exclusion of up to $125,000 of gain.

So, the appraisals were obtained and the federal and state estate tax returns were filed. Although no estate tax was owed, the tax returns established a record of the stepped-up basis at time of death. Some may think this to be a *waste of time,* but there was a *potential future income tax benefit* from documenting the date-of-death value of the portion owned by the deceased spouse (the stepped-up basis at time of death). This made the paper chase necessary and worthwhile.

Money-Saving Suggestion

If you are a surviving spouse, establish the value of your home at the time of your deceased spouse's death by having a realtor give you a written appraisal. This way, if you ever sell the home, you will either not owe any tax or you will *pay a tax that is no greater than the law requires.* Do this even if the assets were owned jointly with your spouse; and do it even though there is no estate tax to pay.

POWERS IN TRUST

Suppose you wish to leave money or other property to someone who is now an infant? There are a few alternatives.

You can use a *testamentary trust.* In your will you might decide to set up the trust as follows:

> I leave $100,000 to ABC Bank as Trustee, to hold the money in trust for my grandson, John Doe; the ABC Bank is to accumulate the income until John Doe is eighteen years old (or whatever age you like); then ABC Bank is to distribute the entire amount to John Doe.

Rather than having the income accumulate, you can direct your trustee to distribute the income, or even the principal, to the minor if he or she is responsible, or to the parent of the minor, or to anyone who provides a service to John. Upon your death, the money will be held by the ABC Bank, as Trustee, until John Doe is whatever age you choose. Suppose that at the time of your death, John has already reached the age you specified in the trust? He will receive the legacy, without it ever being held by a trust.

An alternative is to bequeath the $100,000 *outright* to John Doe, believing that he will have reached adulthood at the time of your death (far in the future). But if he is still a minor when you die, then someone (usually called a *guardian*) will be appointed by a court to supervise the money. This supervision will continue until John Doe reaches the age of majority. Be aware of these two points about a guardianship: a guardian costs money, and the person serving as guardian might be a stranger who intrudes into John Doe's life.

If the testator neither wants to *establish a testamentary trust in his will* nor wants *the court to appoint a guardian,* I recommend the following *powers in trust clause* in the will. Your attorney can explain the rules of your state regarding powers in trust, but this is how it generally works: You give your executor the power to hold the legacy of a minor until the minor reaches the age of majority. You also give the executor the power to apply this money for the benefit of the minor.

I recommend that your will contain a powers in trust clause, even if all your primary legatees are adults. Remember that you have (or should have) alternate legatees named in the will. Although you might leave everything you own to your adult son, John, your will might direct that everything is left to his daughter if he predeceases you. If John, in fact, predeceases you, your legatee may be John's infant daughter. In this case, the powers in trust clause avoids the appointment of a guardian. The upcoming sample situation provides a powers in trust clause.

Sample Situation

Here is a powers in trust clause, which I include in most wills:

> If any person should be under the age of majority when he or she shall become entitled to a legacy or a share of my estate or of any terminating or partially terminating trust, such legacy or share (hereinafter referred to in this Article as the "share") shall vest absolutely in such minor notwithstanding minority. However, my executor may, in his discretion, retain custody of such share until such minor attains the age of majority. My executor, if he decides to retain custody of such share, shall pay or apply so much or all of the income or principal to *or for the benefit of* such minor as he deems necessary or desirable, regardless of any other source or sources of income or support which the minor may have, adding any income not so paid or applied to principal annually. When such minor shall attain the age of majority, the then principal of such share, together with any accumulated income thereon, shall be paid over to such minor. If such minor shall die before attaining the age of majority, then, upon the death of such minor, the then principal of such share, together with any accumulated income thereon, shall be paid over to the estate of such minor.
>
> In making payments to or on behalf of such minor, my executor may make payment directly to such minor if he deems such minor to be of reasonable age and competence, to make application directly to the use of the minor or to make payment to a parent of the minor, to a guardian of the minor appointed in this state or in any other jurisdiction, to a custodian (including any executor hereunder) for such minor under the Uniform Gifts to Minors Act of this state or any other jurisdiction (whether appointed by any executor hereunder or any other person), or to any adult person with whom the minor resides or who has the care or custody of the minor temporarily or permanently.

Money-Saving Suggestion

If you do not want to use a testamentary trust for a legacy to someone who is a minor (perhaps because *you want to avoid the expense of
a trust,* or you think *you will not die before the child reaches majority*),
then consider having a powers in trust clause. This suggestion might save
your estate the cost of an additional court proceeding to appoint a guardian,
and the cost of paying the guardian.

DISINHERITING THOSE WHO OBJECT

You may have a concern that a particular person might attempt to challenge
your will after your death. Unfortunately, there is no sure way to prevent
your will from being challenged; it's one of those "rights" that all distributees
have, and some choose to exercise. One practical way to approach the
question of potential challenges is to forget about it; just have confidence
that your will is legally sufficient to withstand any and all attempts to
contest it.

   However, in many states there is something that can be done to
discourage a potential challenger from exerting the right to contest a will.
By inserting a clause such as the following (which is referred to by the
Latin words *in terrorem,* meaning "by way of warning"), the potential
challenger may have second thoughts about contesting the will:

> If any legatee under this my will, or any codicil hereto, shall, in any man-
> ner, directly or indirectly, attempt to contest or oppose the probate or
> validity of this my will, or any codicil hereto, in any court, or commence
> or prosecute any legal proceeding of any kind in any court to set aside
> this my will, or any codicil hereto, then and in that event such legatee
> shall forfeit and cease to have any right or interest whatsoever under this
> my will, or under any codicil hereto, or in any portion of my estate,
> and in such event, I hereby direct that my property and estate shall be
> disposed of in all respects as if such legatee had predeceased me.

   Along with this clause, your will leaves the next of kin whom you
dislike (and whom you fear is a potential challenger) a sum of money.
Here is an example to help you undersand why a "sum of money" is
bequeathed: Assume that widow Mary has two next of kin, her good
son George and her bad son Brian. Her total worth consists of a money

market account with a balance of $100,000. She leaves $15,000 to Brian, and includes an *in terrorem* clause in her will. Might Brian contest the will? If he does so and *wins,* he receives his intestate share of $50,000; but *if he loses, he receives nothing* (because the will, now approved by the court, conditions his $15,000 legacy on *his not contesting the will).* The $15,000 is the enticement that might be just enough to dissuade him from contesting the will. Brian might be willing to accept the $15,000, and not contest the will.

However, give careful consideration to using this approach because it is a form of succumbing to blackmail. In my example, the widow Mary has left $15,000 to Brian, hoping that he will accept this legacy rather than try to defeat the will and receive his intestate share of $50,000. Perhaps Mary should not worry so much about Brian—and leave him nothing. I also suggest that widow Mary put good George's name on the money market account as the "in trust for" (i.t.f.) beneficiary; and this money goes to George, even if the will is contested successfully. But Mary should also have a will leaving everything to George, just in case she withdraws the money from the money market account, purchases a certificate of deposit, and *forgets to put George's name on the certificate of deposit.* She should also have a will naming George the residuary legatee, in case she *wins the lottery.*

Sample Situations

Earlier on we learned about living trusts, called *inter vivos trusts* (see chapter 8). Those who anticipate that a disinherited next of kin might be a potential challenger to the will might give some thought to establishing a living trust. A bank (or perhaps even you) can serve as trustee; you can transfer your assets to this trustee; *and* you can be the beneficiary of the trust. The trust instrument names who succeeds you as trustee after your death, and specifies who receives the trust funds at your death. The assets in the trust avoid probate at the time of your death. However, as you have learned throughout this book, these assets in the trust are still included as part of your taxable estate.

Why is this procedure preferred by some people, rather than having the estate distributed by the will? Well, it does eliminate the challenges of lack of testamentary capacity, fraud, duress, and undue influence that can be aimed at a will. If you establish this trust, and you receive distributions of money from this trust until your death some years later, it is difficult for your disinherited heir to argue successfully that you did not know what you were doing. After all, you were living with this trust from perhaps age seventy until perhaps age ninety-two.

Another way of decreasing the chances of a will challenge is to make gifts of your assets to those you love, thereby *reducing the value of your eventual estate* (although, as you learned in chapter 17, there might be a gift tax owed by you). This is a dramatic approach, because once the gift has been given, you have *no legal right to get it back.* There are cases, however, of people giving away money, motivated by their dislike of a relative who may challenge a will if there is money available in an estate.

Money-Saving Suggestion

Give consideration to establishing a *living trust.* It saves probate costs, and it lessens the chances of aggressive relatives picking over your estate. These trusts are particularly popular in California, Florida, Illinois, Massachusetts, and Ohio. I am only suggesting that you consider this approach; you may decide against it. I do not want to further complicate your life—e.g., by suggesting that you have all your assets in a trust—unless you are certain that your particular situation warrants the paperwork and the attorney's fee. On the other hand, you may want to establish this *living trust.* You *are* in control.

A LEGATEE WHO MIGHT GET DIVORCED

Divorce is a fact of life. Many people, therefore, have the following concern: "I'm leaving my son everything, but I'm so afraid that he and his wife will get divorced after I die; in the divorce settlement she will get half of whatever I might leave my son."

There are a couple of ways to approach this problem. One strategy is to act like an ostrich, put your head in the sand, *and just do not worry about this problem.* I am being completely serious here. Sometimes worrying about your child's possible divorce can actually be a self-fulfilling prophecy. What you are doing is projecting onto your child your dislike of the chosen mate. While parents should not be blamed for everything (and perhaps they should be blamed for nothing), some parents can be blamed for a child's divorce. They convince a weak person that this is the anticipated outcome.

A more profound bit of advice would be to leave your child the legacy *in trust*. Consider giving your trustee the discretion to distribute or withhold income. We will consider this more closely in the next sample situation.

But realize that you can never have a perfect plan for the distribution of your assets after death. I believe that this quest for the perfect distribution of assets is, ironically, part of the reason so many people die without a will. Years of thought and worry result in a paralysis of decision-making ability. Thinking about death is what makes the preparation of a will difficult in itself; do not make matters worse for yourself by seeking perfection. *Structure* a plan, *discuss* it with your attorney, *prepare* the will, *review* it every year or two—this is all anyone can or should do.

Sample Situation

The various states have developed their own laws determining the economic consequence of divorce on concepts of fairness. Alimony, the periodic payment of money from the richer spouse to the poorer spouse, is being supplemented or substituted by equitable distribution. With *equitable distribution,* each spouse can receive one-half of all the assets acquired during the marriage—maybe more or less than one-half depending on the history of the marriage. But what if one spouse is the beneficiary of a trust?

A judge might react unsympathetically to the beneficiary of a substantial trust, and decide that this spouse is not in *need* of support (or perhaps able to *provide greater support* to the other spouse). However, if distributions from the trust are at the discretion of the trustee, the spouse/beneficiary would impress upon the court that future distributions are *not a sure thing*.

Money-Saving Suggestion

Rather than worrying about your legatee's marriage and whether or not this legacy should be put in trust, consider the possibility that your own marriage may disintegrate. A nuptial agreement with your spouse, which we discussed earlier in chapter 2, may be needed. This agreement can cover two situations: *if divorced,* what are the financial obligations of each spouse; if there is a *death* of a spouse, should the surviving spouse receive the minimal spousal share (the elective share that we also discussed in chapter 2), or are the spouses waiving this right. Think about it.

This worry about your legatee who might get divorced centers on a word that often appears in discussions of estate planning—*control.* The hand from the grave can exercise some control, but there is a limit. My suggestion is that you worry less. Of course, a trust in the will is the control that sometimes is required.

POWER OF ATTORNEY; CONSERVATOR

You are probably familiar with a *power of attorney*. Simply stated, person A gives person B the rights of A, such as the right to withdraw A's money from a bank. It may be a *general power of attorney*, where B is treated in every situation as if B were A. For example, B can sell A's home or withdraw money from A's bank accounts. Or it can be a *limited power of attorney*, where B can legally bind A to just one transaction (or perhaps a few). For example, B is only authorized to have a power of attorney for a particular bank account.

There is a clause, called a *durable power* clause, that can be included with a power of attorney. This clause states that the power will remain in force *even if the person giving the power becomes mentally incompetent*. There is even a clause, called a *springing power* clause, that says the power is only *effective if and when the person giving the power becomes mentally incompetent*. There is no power of attorney, however, that *continues after the death of the person granting the power*.

If you are the person *giving* a power of attorney, be careful. You must have great trust in the person to whom you give your power. Be careful as well if you are the person *receiving* a power of attorney. If an old and sick person gives you a power, realize that you may have to answer for all your actions on behalf of that person. Remember reading in chapter 15 about the responsibility of the executor to act prudently or else risk the consequences of personal financial liability for every imprudence? The same standard applies here. You may be questioned years later; you cannot then say that this old and sick person authorized and supervised all your actions. Even if not actually stated in the power of attorney, implicit in the *authorization* is that you act *prudently*. What is also implicit is that your control of the money was not *supervised;* the enfeebled person gave you this control *only because unassisted financial management was no longer possible*.

A *conservator* is a person appointed by a court to represent a person who cannot manage his or her financial affairs. In some states the conservator goes under another title, such as guardian. A doctor usually is required to testify in court as to whether the person whose affairs are to be supervised is able to manage alone. The person who petitions to become a conservator is questioned by the court on both motive and ability. A conservator is appointed only after unequivocal evidence has been presented to the court that a conservator is necessary. A *committee* has more extensive legal significance than a conservator. A committee is a person who not only manages the finances but also has the authority and responsibility to act in all matters on behalf of the incapacitated person. The appointment of the committee results in the loss of civil rights of the incapacitated person.

Let us compare the function of a conservator with that of a holder of a power of attorney. It is safer to be a conservator because your actions are reviewed by the court periodically (usually annually). With a power of attorney you are acting all alone, and are a target for those who may later want to question your conduct. This is the subject of our next sample situation.

Sample Situations

Looking at the interests of the *person receiving a power of attorney,* it is better to be appointed a conservator than to control another person's finances with a power of attorney (unless it is just for a short time, such as during a hospitalization). Imagine holding a person's power of attorney for six years, and then having someone ask you to account for every penny of *principal* and *investment income,* including interest, dividends, gains or losses, for the past six years. Someone who possesses a power of attorney for another individual may one day have to present such an accounting on how the incapacitated person's assets were invested and spent. Even if you were bonded, that wouldn't help *you.* Bonding is protection for *the person whose money you are managing.* If the bonding company has to make good on your mistakes, it will. It will then proceed to collect this money from you.

Looking at the interests of the *person giving a power of attorney,* it can be risky since great trust is being placed in another individual. The person you trust might be dishonest or reckless or generally incompetent. Be independent for as long as possible. There are alternatives, like an emergency joint bank account with a friend (which is described in the next money-saving suggestion), to assist in this regard.

The form for transferring power of attorney can be obtained at most stationery stores, but I recommend that you discuss its use with your attorney. In some situations a power of attorney *is appropriate.* But proceed cautiously. Incidentally, if you want to give someone power over a particular bank account, the bank most likely requires that you use the bank's power of attorney form.

Money-Saving Suggestion

A client of advanced age who lived alone asked me if I had any suggestions on how to assure that her bills would be paid if she were hospitalized for a short period of time. She was particularly concerned about her rent, utility, and medical insurance bills. I advised her to have a joint bank account with a friend or relative and to give this person the right to withdraw funds. Because the friend is able to withdraw money from the account, I advised her to leave only about $2,500 in the account. The friend could then pay the bills with money withdrawn from the joint account. *This procedure avoids the problem of unpaid bills when you are in the hospital for a short stay.* It alleviates the fears that you might be evicted, that your telephone service might be disrupted, or that the grace period for late payment of an insurance premium might expire. In some situations there is no need to transfer power of attorney or establish a conservator *if you follow my joint bank account suggestion.*

MOURNING ACCOUNT

Some elderly folks have a worry about paying their funeral bill. This is a serious worry, one that cannot be put to rest by commenting, tongue in cheek, that the funeral director will not be able to sue you. For those who are concerned about these expenses, here are a few suggestions.

I recommend that you tell your friend, whose name is on that *small bank account,* that these funds are to be used not only to pay bills during an emergency, such as your hospitalization, but also for funeral expenses. If you are not comfortable with this recommendation, perhaps one of the following suggestions will assist you.

Since you obviously trust your executor (by giving this person the legal right to control all your assets after your death), consider opening *a savings account in your executor's name.* Deposit enough money in it to cover the anticipated funeral expenses.

Prepay the funeral expenses. This helps to assure that your burial wishes are carried out. However, make sure your executor has the receipt from the funeral home (and, as you first learned in chapter 5, make sure your *executor is fully informed of your burial wishes*). Keep in mind that the amount paid is perhaps just an estimate. But maybe the funeral home will agree to a fixed price, and any increased cost as a result of inflation will be offset by the interest the funeral home will have received on the money you paid.

You might also get some relief by realizing that a funeral home does not always require *instant payment*. It will give your closest relative, or your executor, a short period of time in which to gather the estate's assets and thus have money available for payment of this final bill.

Have you thought of *cremation?* It is not expensive, and it is the funeral of choice for more and more people. Cremation and a memorial service, in my opinion, is an appropriate way to go. A memorial service is a general reaffirmation of the worth of life and a review of the particular individual's basic goodness.

If you have a worry about your funeral bill, then resolve the problem now, and *never let it bother you again.*

Sample Situation

There are cases of people who die and no one knows whom to contact. Perhaps the body is discovered by the superintendent in the building where the deceased resided. Perhaps the person died while living in a shelter for the homeless. In these cases the community's public administrator takes care of the burial. *This is what is feared by some senior citizens.* It is not only the question of the payment for the final disposition of the body, but also whether the body is *claimed and put to rest*.

Families are now spread throughout the country, and even the world. The case of the elderly person who lives alone is not a unique one. However, the problem of claiming the body and putting it to rest is really the least important of quite a few problems that this elderly person encounters. Far more serious are the problems of *loneliness* (which often, but not necessarily, results from being alone), *health maintenance,* and *housing.* I believe that an appropriate standard by which to judge the decency of a society is the manner in which its elderly are treated. It is unfortunate that Congressman Claude Pepper of Florida is no longer with us. I am optimistic, however, that other members of Congress will champion the cause of senior citizens and that the political power of older persons will continue to grow. Senior citizens are dedicated voters, and if demographic studies are correct, their numbers are dramatically increasing. Eventually, Congress will have to respond.

Money-Saving Suggestion

My suggestions to senior citizens who are alone include: try to develop a *friendship* with someone, perhaps someone who also is alone; join a *social group* in your neighborhood, perhaps at your church or synagogue; express your aloneness to a *relative,* and see if there is any expression of support; explore the possibility of relocating to a *senior citizen* housing development (but not to a nursing home); if you are able, *volunteer* your time to a favorite charity.

Bob Hope, in delivering a commencement address, gave this advice to those going out into the world: *don't go.* To those thinking about entering a nursing home, I give the same advice. The loss of independence is overwhelming; the nursing home alternative should be chosen only after all other reasonable options have been explored and rejected.

LIFE INSURANCE

One purpose of life insurance is to *pay any estate tax.* This is a particular need if an individual owns assets that are not liquid (for example, a building). It may be difficult for an estate to pay the estate tax without selling or mortgaging the asset.

Of course there are other important reasons for life insurance. *Through life insurance, survivors who relied upon a deceased's income can continue to live with financial security.* The period after death is a difficult time for the survivors. Surely it is not the time for them to cope with financial difficulties.

Both spouses should be insured, particularly in double-income families. If there is a dependent child, the amount of insurance needed can be substantial. This is especially true if one spouse has a job involving travel. Imagine if the nontraveling spouse were to die. What would be the cost of an around-the-clock, live-in helper? Maybe the cost of a larger home should also be anticipated, because of the extra space needed for the live-in helper. Explore your insurance needs. The cost of adequate insurance protection is well worth it.

There are two basic types of life insurance: *term insurance* and *whole-life insurance*. With term insurance, you pay the premium, and if you do not die during the term of the policy (usually one year), then you happily have lost your investment. Whole-life insurance, which is more expensive than term insurance, gives you life-insurance protection and a cash build-up in the policy. There are variations on term and whole-life insurance (including survivor whole-life insurance), which your insurance advisor can explain to you. After you have purchased insurance, remember to increase the coverage periodically to keep up with both your higher standard of living and inflation.

Sample Situation

Someone said to me that he was too poor to afford insurance. *The irony is that the poorer you are the greater your need for life insurance.* This is because your survivor will not be receiving any legacy from you, and the loss of your income may be followed by a period of increased expenses. It is difficult to solve the problem of being poor. But life insurance is one way to ease the burden on your survivors. Life insurance should be on your priority list of investments.

Money-Saving Suggestion

Perhaps the *beneficiary* of a life insurance policy should be *the owner of the policy.* Here is one way to keep a life insurance payout free from estate tax:

There is $100,000 of life insurance on Mary's life, and the proceeds are payable to John. *John owns the policy and pays the premium.* This way, Mary's total estate does not include the $100,000.

You can also have a trust own the policy. *This saves estate tax when the insured dies, ana also when the primary beneficiary dies.* Here is how you implement this suggestion:

There is $100,000 of life insurance on Mary's life, and the proceeds are payable to *an irrevocable trust that owns the policy (ideally, from its inception) and pays the premium.* The trust receives the $100,000 upon Mary's death. The trust agreement directs that John is to receive the income from the $100,000 for the rest of his life. The trust agreement also directs who eventually is to receive the $100,000 upon John's death. This way, neither Mary's estate nor John's estate includes the $100,000 of insurance proceeds.

Keep in mind, however, that an insurance policy, such as a whole life policy, has a *value* to it. For example, if *John owns* the policy that *insures Mary's life,* then, upon *John's death,* his estate will include the value of this policy. Consult your insurance advisor. Also, compare the premiums of different companies; there is a difference among carriers. Inquire as to whether the policy is automatically renewed each year, or whether you are required to have periodic physicals. If you are a smoker, I urge that you give it up; not only will you feel better, your life insurance premium is lower because your life expectancy is longer.

COMMON DISASTER

A common disaster is relevant to a discussion of wills because people dying in the disaster may have an interest in each other's estates. These situations are not so unusual; they can occur when there are tragedies such as fires, automobile collisions, or airline crashes, any of which could result in multiple deaths of family members.

Let us take the example of an aunt who is leaving her entire estate to her niece. Perhaps they are the closest of friends, travel extensively together, and generally share their lives. Therefore, there is a chance that they will die together, perhaps when traveling. For the aunt's will, here are two recommendations that might be considered:

As mentioned at the start of this book, it is always good to have a *successor legatee.* Although the aunt's will leaves all the rest, residue, and remainder of her estate to her niece, the will should also state to whom the property goes if the niece predeceases the aunt.

The aunt's will should also have a clause (called a *common disaster clause* or a *simultaneous death clause*) such as the following: "If any beneficiary under this my Will and I should die in a common disaster or under such conditions that it would be difficult or impossible to determine which of us died first, then such beneficiary shall be deemed for the purposes of this Will to have *predeceased me.*" This way, if the aunt and niece die together, the aunt's assets go to the successor legatee named in the aunt's will, and not the legatees of the niece.

Suppose the aunt decides to have the simultaneous death clause state the opposite presumption; that is, if she and the niece die together, then the aunt is deemed as having predeceased the niece. The aunt's estate is then distributed to those named in the *niece's will.* If the niece does not have a will, the aunt's estate goes to the *niece's next of kin.* With respect to my example, I know of no reason for the aunt to make this choice.

If you have a common disaster clause in your will, read it. Learn which choice *you* made; find out *why* this choice was made. In summary: you control where your assets go if *your legatee has predeceased you* by having named a *successor legatee;* furthermore, you are also controlling where your money goes if *you and your legatee die together* by having a *common disaster clause* in your will.

Sample Situations

In the case of simultaneous death of a married couple, the common disaster clause is crucial.

The first case to look at is the married couple, *without children from this marriage,* who are killed in an accident. Suppose, for example, that the wife survives the husband by a few minutes. Unless your state has a law dealing with this situation, or unless the *husband's* will has a common disaster clause, those named in the *wife's* will (or in the absence of a will, the wife's next of kin) receive the husband's assets as well as the wife's assets. This is significant for the couple without children, because the *husband's and wife's successor legatees might not be the same people.* It is also significant for a couple where there is a child or children from a *previous marriage.* Although each spouse might leave everything to the other, the wife might leave everything to her nieces and nephews (or a child from a previous marriage), in the event that her husband predeceases her. The husband, on the other hand, might leave everything to his nieces and nephews (or a child from a previous marriage) if his wife predeceases him.

Another case to consider is that of the wealthy couple. For tax reasons, the will of the wealthier spouse might state that the other spouse is the survivor in the event of a common disaster. This is particularly important if only one spouse has assets in excess of $600,000. This couple has to plan this clause carefully, as well as every aspect of the will, to utilize fully the opportunity to have up to $600,000 pass tax free through the *poorer spouse's estate.* Pages could be written about this situation; if it applies to you, I leave it to your attorney to explain how this tax savings is achieved.

Money-Saving Suggestion

Do not rely on state law to cover the situation of common disaster; have a simultaneous death clause in your will. Your legatee may die with you in an accident. In most situations you do not want this legacy ultimately to be distributed to this person's legatees or next of kin.

NONMARITAL RELATIONSHIPS

Suppose you want to leave your estate to someone you love, but you are aware that your closest relatives *do not approve* of this person. Perhaps it is a homosexual relationship, a heterosexual relationship not sanctioned by marriage, or an interracial relationship. Perhaps other people close to you do not believe this person is worthy to live with such *perfection embodied by the one and only you.* Here is what you can do:

Your bankbooks and other investments can have your friend's name on them; use either the *in trust for* or *joint account with right of survivorship* forms of ownership. (Once again, this assures that the asset goes to the other person on the account and is not distributed through your will. However, it does not remove this asset from your taxable estate.)

Have a *will* prepared; leave your assets to this person if that is your wish.

Have a clause in the will—the *in terrorem clause* discussed earlier — stating that if a person challenges the will, this person receives nothing.

Finally, if you are suffering from a terminal illness, you might want to make a *gift* of your assets to the one you love. File a gift tax return if necessary (as you know, it is necessary if the gift exceeds $10,000). Be sure to unequivocally deliver the gift to the recipient, and make sure the recipient unequivocally accepts the gift. This is how your attorney would advise you. But your attorney would conclude with this serious and practical warning: once the gift is given, *you have no recourse to reclaim it.* The seriousness of this situation is twofold: the gift might be all your money, and it might be money that is desperately needed for medical treatment. *Proceed cautiously.*

Estate problems often occur when the deceased has died of AIDS (Acquired Immune Deficiency Syndrome). Family members are judgmental of the person remembered in the will.

Sample Situation

Do not confuse highly publicized palimony cases with estate cases. Palimony cases occur when former friends split, and they are fighting between themselves. Estate cases on nontraditional relationships occur when *the friend of the deceased receives the deceased's assets, and the family of the deceased questions the will.*

What the will says is almost always what happens. *So make sure there is a will.* Without a will (or an "in trust for" account or "joint account with right of survivorship" or a "living trust"), the most loved person has no chance of receiving a thing.

Money-Saving Suggestion

Severe family disruption can occur over items possessing virtually no economic value. As the combatants often state, it is the principle of the matter that is important. More likely, it is a deep-rooted problem that erupts over a question as trivial as "Who gets the five-cent refundable cans owned by the deceased?" A costly will contest can result.

Furniture is often a contested area. Here is a suggestion for two people living together. Both should have a list of what each owns; the list should state how ownership was obtained and that there is no intention of making a gift of furniture to family members. This helps to avoid two problems: the potential claim of a family member that the furniture of the deceased was never owned by the deceased, but only *loaned* to the person by this family member; and conversely, the potential claim of a family member of the deceased that, during the final illness, the deceased gave the furniture as a *gift* to the family member.

Another suggestion for cases in which a will challenge is imminent is to *videotape the signing of the will.* The film might then be admissible as evidence to show testamentary capacity. However, videotaping the signing of a will is a new development and there are some possible dangers. For example, the terminally ill person might appear so debilitated on film that the videotape might do more harm than good. Nevertheless, videotaping the signing of the will is something to consider.

TOO RICH FOR MEDICAID

The poor qualify for medical assistance through the government program known as Medicaid. "Poor" means "very poor," a net worth of less than approximately $4,750 and minimal income. There is not much you can do about the government's definition of "poor." There is, however, something that you can do to decrease your net worth. *Give gifts!*

The tactic of giving gifts, and thus becoming poor enough to qualify for government assistance, can present a minefield of problems. I recommend legal advice, but here are some things to consider:

Apply for Medicaid no sooner than *three years* after the gifts are made. I recommend that tax returns be filed, even if the income is *below the amount that triggers the filing requirement.* It provides evidence of little or no income. Also, check with your attorney to be sure that the three-year period has remained the minimum interval between gift-giving and qualification for Medicaid.

Most people will not make large gifts, so *proceed diplomatically* if you suggest to an older family member that gift-giving may allow eventual Medicaid eligibility. That person's accumulated money is the product of a lifetime of hard work and is not readily given away.

Some people are happier giving money to a nursing home than to a relative, particularly to a relative who asks for a gift. Some people believe that *better medical and nursing service is rendered* when the patient, rather than the government, is making the payment. Some people also believe that a *stigma is attached to welfare payments,* and thus they will not apply for Medicaid. In most situations the nursing home employees who provide the care *do not know whether the patient or the government is paying.* As for stigmatizing a Medicaid recipient, remember that many of them have paid *quite a lot of taxes over the years* as well as having made *other valuable contributions* to our society. If a society cannot, or worse *will not,* provide for the *poorest* among its *oldest* citizens, then this society will not long endure.

Move slowly, carefully, in good taste, and with advice of wise counsel. You may have heard stories where money was given away to meet Medicaid qualifications. Either a crime was committed by defrauding the government with a false answer to the "were gifts made" question on the Medicaid application, or some careful legal planning was successfully implemented.

Sample Situation

Doctors' bills, nursing home charges, home care expenses, medication, and all the other health-related costs incurred by the aged and sick patient may total a tremendous sum of money. Four suggestions might help you avoid this calamity: do your best to *stay healthy,* pay for a very comprehensive medical *insurance policy,* give *gifts* of your money, and consider having a *living will.*

A sample situation on gifts that I remember most vividly concerned a person who asked me if I would speak to his elderly female relative who was leaving everything to him. He wanted her to start making gifts to him, because he was afraid medical expenses would substantially erode, or perhaps even eliminate, her assets. When I asked where the relative lived, he responded, without any embarrassment, "Somewhere in New Jersey, I haven't been out there in quite a while." I advised him that there was no chance of receiving a gift, and that such a request might jeopardize his legacy.

Money-Saving Suggestions

Gifts made by a person who is relatively well off can make that person poor enough to qualify for government aid. I recommend these gifts, however, only where there is a loving family relationship that has existed for many years. The successful instances of this gift-giving technique are where the family member is *presently living with the potential recipients of the gift.* The person making the gift is reciprocating the love already shown by other family members. The eventual qualification for Medicaid is a possible family bonus some years later.

Do not make such gifts when the door of the hospital is being opened. The gifts should be made when the giver is still relatively healthy. A few years should elapse before applying for Medicaid. *The applicant for Medicaid must explain to the government all gifts made within a few years prior to the application.* Unless the explanation shows some extraordinary circumstances for gifts made shortly before applying for Medicaid (and I cannot think of any example), the applicant will not be considered eligible.

SELLING YOUR RESIDENCE

The most valuable asset in many estates is the family residence. There are two concerns associated with the sale of a home, *taxes* and *emotions.*
    I offer four ideas on the *tax consequences* of selling your home:

If you sell your home and *buy (bought) or build (built) a new one within a time period specified in the tax law* (currently *two years,* so I will use two years when referring to this time period), the entire profit from the sale is tax deferred if your replacement residence costs more than the adjusted sales price of your old home. This applies to everyone, regardless of age.

If you are over the age of fifty-five, up to $125,000 of profit from the sale might be exempt from tax, even if you do not buy or build a new home within two years. *This is a tax break that can be used only once in a lifetime.*

If you do not buy or build a new residence within two years and you do not qualify for the over age fifty-five treatment, *your profit from the sale is taxed just like regular income.*

The stepped-up basis that your heirs will receive at the time of your death might be a tax reason for you to hold onto your home. This situation exists if the home has appreciated in value by more than $125,000 and also if a new residence is not going to be purchased. Therefore, if you sell it (and do not defer payment of the tax by buying a new home), you will pay a tax on the portion of your gain exceeding $125,000. By holding onto it *until your death,* both you and your heirs avoid any tax on the increase in value in the home.

    The *emotional problem* associated with selling a residence is that the home might be too big for its one or two occupants. Some readers may be in the highly emotional state known as the *empty nest syndrome:* the children are grown, and now the big house seems so empty. This loneliness is extremely severe if a loved one has recently died, so the idea of selling the home is considered. *But do not act in haste.* In the next few pages we will explore the emotional and social costs of selling the residence and moving, but first a sample situation and a money-saving suggestion.

Sample Situation

To help you understand the following money-saving suggestion, here is a quick legal description of a cooperative (co-op) apartment and a condominium (condo) apartment.

In a co-op the building is owned by a corporation, and you buy shares of stock in this corporation. You are given a lease (called a proprietary lease) to the apartment you occupy. If the building has a mortgage, you pay a portion of the cost of the mortgage. *In a condo you actually own a piece of real property,* which is your apartment. There is usually no mortgage on the building. It is easier to sell a condo because, unlike a co-op, you do not have to ask the neighbors (serving as the building's directors) to approve a potential buyer.

Money-Saving Suggestion

As you know, if you sell your residence and buy or build a new one within two years, you can defer paying any tax on the entire profit from the sale. However, to defer paying a tax on the entire profit, you must replace your residence with a more expensive home than the one you sold. Here is a thought for someone who has sold a home and has bought a cooperative apartment. The cost of the new apartment includes not only what you pay the seller, but also the *amount of mortgage on the building* attributed to your percentage of ownership of the corporation that owns the building. Here is an example:

A home that was purchased a few years ago for $40,000 is sold at $100,000, for a profit of $60,000. In order to defer a tax on this $60,000 profit, a new home must be bought or built for at least $100,000 within two years. Suppose a new home is bought for only $80,000? Then there is a current tax on $20,000 of the profit. But if a co-op is purchased for $80,000, the portion of the building mortgage assumed by the buyer is added to the purchase price of $80,000, and perhaps this additional amount increases the total cost to $100,000 or more.

With the popularity of co-op apartments, perhaps you will encounter this situation. Since a *condo* usually does not have a mortgage on the building, it is rare that this situation applies.

RELOCATING

States of preference for people who choose to retire have included Arizona, California, Florida, Kentucky, North Carolina, and South Carolina. I advise you to think twice before you move to the promised land of sun and fun for seniors. The best place to retire might be right where you are now living. The emotional trauma of relocating is double-barreled: the upheaval of *making the move* is followed by the uncertainty of *establishing an identity* in the new community.

As for the move itself, it is not the one-day affair when the movers arrive and load the truck. It is many months of sorting out, throwing out, and reliving a lifetime of memories. It is a round of saying goodbye to those who are close to you and, interestingly enough, those you recently discovered are close to you. You are saying goodbye to your roots: friends, shopkeepers, bankers, ministers, and family members who have decided not to relocate. *Any retired person I have ever spoken to about this move has expressed feelings of loss and pain.*

The second part of the trauma is establishing an identity in the new location—different people, different climate, a new and different life. Perhaps this is not the stage of life to start a new existence. Remember the Tom Dooley television advertisement where he exhorted the viewers to come on down. (Where? Florida!) Looking back on this advertisement, I now realize that it was a promise of a fountain of youth; the advertisement showed the youngest retirees I have ever seen. Older Americans went, while younger Americans counted the years until retirement.

Give some thought (and I mean a year of thought) to relocating after a spouse or close relative dies. The time of grief is not the time to make such a dramatic change. Many times we take life's pleasures for granted. The friendly local merchants, the friendships developed over the years, the memberships in a church group or social club, and the characters who bring the community to life—they are all a significant part of your life. For the older person, particularly one who has lost a loved one, the security of familiarity is important. *Relocation can be exhilarating but also traumatic.*

Sample Situation

I was recently told of a couple who had lived in their home for forty-eight years, decided to retire, and purchased a new home *without even seeing it*. They relied on pictures and on the glowing description of the leisurely life in this retirement heaven. The person telling me the story was surprised and saddened. These were his parents' next door neighbors, and he had known them his whole life, keeping in contact with them even after he married and moved away from home. He said that they were a part of his life, and when they moved he felt sad for them, for his parents, and for himself. To think they moved without even seeing their new home! Surprise was not my reaction.

The retirement move has been reinforced by advertising, which seductively entices retired people to find happiness *elsewhere* by crossing the River Jordan and entering the promised land. When the time comes that the body is older and wearier, there is a greater susceptibility to this preconditioned idea that a different location is what the older body needs. *Perhaps where you are now living is the best location for your retirement.*

Money-Saving Suggestions

Before you make a decision on permanent relocation, *take a vacation for a few months in the retirement community of your dreams.* The extra expense of renting accommodations for this long vacation may prove to be worthwhile. During this vacation you can decide whether the dream is reality. If it really is a dream come true, then relocate; if not, you have saved yourself some heartache and some money.

Here is something I learned from a client who had recently retired. If you live in a large city, *become a tourist in your city:* visit the museums, the stores, and the local attractions. If your city has a sightseeing bus tour, take it. At least get to know your city, or perhaps reacquaint yourself with your city before you relocate. Maybe you will like it. Maybe you will even stay!

ON BEING A WIDOW OR WIDOWER

In some families, one of the spouses is the dominating force on budgeting and investing. My overall experience among clients has been that this chore is pretty much gender neutral. With some older clients, however, this division of labor sometimes slants more to the husband.

Both spouses should understand money. One of the spouses will out-live the other, and it is difficult when the less knowledgeable money manager is the survivor. Therefore, start sharing your knowledge of money with your spouse. Both husbands and wives should know their stockbroker, their banker, their insurance agent, and their trusted family attorney. Each should know the family's monthly cost of living, and each should know how to manage the family budget. A great development in education has been the proliferation of adult education courses. Take a few of these courses together, particularly on financial management. By planning now, the eventual survivor of your marriage will be able to cope with the return to single life.

You have just been reading about money, and whether a widow or widower can handle money. But the far greater problems encountered by widows and widowers are *emotional in nature*. They have to cope with feelings of anger, regret, and loneliness. The *anger* may be directed at the deceased spouse, God, the physician, relatives, government institutions such as the Social Security Administration, the executor, the attorney, and friends who are perceived as being distant. The plaintive cry is, "Why have I been left alone?" There is *regret* at not having fully shared the good times with the deceased spouse. The survivor wishes that the fulfillment of dreams had not been deferred, because now it is too late. *Loneliness*, along with helplessness, anxiety, and fear, engulfs the surviving spouse, who now must face the future alone. There is also the nagging doubt as to whether solo living is possible.

Sadly, the surviving spouse may try an emotional release through abuse of alcohol or drugs. However, by planning for the eventuality of a spouse's death, you can lessen the pain. Be financially independent; have some individual interests; develop a friendship or two. Most of all, *have confidence that you will survive the pain*. Do not reject a helping hand extended by family members; *you are deserving of this help*.

Sample Situation

There is a story about the married man who had a guilt-provoking clause in his will. He requested to be cremated, to have his ashes mixed in a can full of paint, which would then be used to paint the ceiling of the bedroom.

Perhaps this story elicits a chuckle. But the subject of the story, *guilt*, is both relevant and serious. The guilt felt by the surviving spouse is *self-inflicted* and *unnecessary*. However, it is equally as painful as the guilt-provoking clause in the deceased spouse's will. Often a surviving spouse feels guilty, despite a history of emotional balance. This results from the unanticipated sense of relief that the spouse has died, and this relief is experienced for two reasons. The *surviving* spouse is relieved that the burden of the painstaking care of an ill spouse has finally ended; the surviving spouse is also relieved that the *deceased* spouse is no longer suffering. Such relief is normal and should not be *a source of guilt*. If the surviving widow or widower rejects the helping hand extended by children of the marriage (or other close family members), guilt is often the culprit. An awareness of this problem might help both the surviving spouse and the rejected family members understand why the survivor is sometimes not too cooperative in accepting advice or assistance.

Money-Saving Suggestions

It is never too early to start planning for retirement and the possibility of being the surviving spouse. Plan for both the *economic* and the *emotional* consequences of widowhood. Plan on living retirement as a couple, but also plan for the possibility that you will be the survivor of the marriage.

Learn to be independent. Start today. A *net worth statement* should be prepared; it allows both spouses a clearer view of their financial picture, and it is also a start for when they begin planning eventual retirement. If the couple does not understand money, they should start to learn about it today. Each partner should also develop an interest in some activity in which he or she participates as a solo, not as a member of a couple. These suggestions will somewhat ease the emotional trauma the survivor will experience when the spouse dies.

AN ESTATE TAX REVIEW FOR WEALTHY SPOUSES

There is no estate tax on *any amount received by a spouse* (again, assuming this spouse a United States citizen). After the death of both spouses, however, there is a federal estate tax on everything over $600,000, and the tax starts at 37 percent. For example, suppose the combined net worth of a couple is $700,000. Here is what happens: a spouse dies, and the surviving spouse can receive everything without the payment of any estate tax. When the surviving spouse then dies, the children (or whoever) get everything, and the estate tax is $37,000. Here is a proposed estate plan for this couple with a *total net worth of $700,000;* it shows how this $37,000 estate tax on the estate of the surviving spouse can be avoided:

> Assets in the amount of $500,000 are jointly owned; the husband owns $100,000 individually; and the wife owns $100,000 individually. The husband, through his will, leaves $100,000 to his wife, in trust, and

she will receive the income from this $100,000. The $500,000 belongs to the wife upon the husband's death through the joint ownership. The wife's will is a mirror image of the husband's. The tax benefit is that the $100,000 currently in a trust is not taxed in the eventual estate of the surviving spouse.

Let me repeat the *economic result* of this plan on the *surviving spouse:* the surviving spouse has $600,000 (the $500,000 that had been jointly owned and the $100,000 individually owned), plus the income from the $100,000 trust. Let me repeat the *estate taxation result* on the *estate of the surviving spouse.* This *$100,000* trust is not included in the taxable estate of the second spouse to die, and thus the surviving spouse has a tax-free estate of *$600,000* (the $500,000 that had been jointly owned and the $100,000 individually owned).

As you already learned in chapter 17, a couple can leave up to $1.2 million free of federal estate tax. But how? It is the same trust technique as just suggested to the couple with total assets of $700,000. The husband owns $600,000 individually; the wife owns $600,000 individually; and each leaves everything to the other in a testamentary trust. Upon the death of the first spouse, there is no estate tax; upon the death of the surviving spouse there is no estate tax, because *the $600,000 in the testamentary trust of the first spouse to die is not included in the taxable estate of the surviving spouse.*

Sample Situations

Here are some other estate tax ideas for the wealthy couple who has total assets over $600,000, as learned from case histories of actual couples with substantial assets:

Do nothing. Many spouses want to receive everything; they do not want to be bothered with a trust set up in a will, and they do not worry if there is an estate tax *after they both have died.*

Again do nothing. However, after the first spouse has died, the surviving spouse might consider giving gifts to reduce net worth closer to the $600,000 amount.

Use a trust as explained on the previous page.

A husband and a wife might each consider *increasing the amount left to those other than the spouse,* which is the subject of the following suggestion.

Money-Saving Suggestion

Consider increasing the amount left to *those other than the spouse.* Here is an example:

A husband and wife have a net worth of $700,000. The problem is that after both have died, there will be a $37,000 estate tax. They could own $500,000 of assets jointly. The wife owns $100,000 of assets in her name only; the husband owns $100,000 of assets in his name only. The wife could then leave $100,000 to their (or her) children; her husband receives the $500,000 of jointly owned property if he survives his wife. Similarly, the husband could leave $100,000 to their (or his) children, and his wife receives the $500,000 of jointly owned property if she survives him.

With this suggestion the *surviving spouse* has $600,000 (the $500,000 that had been jointly owned plus the $100,000 individually owned). This plan, rather than the previous plan, has the benefit that *there is no trust;* the detriment is that money is dropped down to the younger generation *while either the husband or wife is still alive.* Some people like this suggestion; others say, "So what if our children have to pay an estate tax!"

SHOULD SPOUSES OWN ASSETS JOINTLY?

Estate tax consequences for wealthy spouses have just been reviewed. Joint ownership was again mentioned. Let's review this option. It is important, and often misunderstood, which could be costly.

If a couple's total net worth is under $600,000, then I generally recommend joint ownership. This way everything goes to the surviving spouse and there is no need to go to court with the will of the first spouse to die. Succinctly and legally stated, *probate is avoided.* There is no federal estate tax either when the first spouse dies or when the surviving spouse dies.

Here are two situations, however, where joint ownership must be avoided:

First, if some money is left in the will to someone other than the spouse, then that person will receive nothing *if a husband and wife jointly own everything*. This occurs because the surviving spouse receives everything through the joint ownership, and there is nothing left to be distributed through the will. Therefore, if a spouse wants to leave $10,000 to a daughter, make sure that the $10,000 is solely owned, that is, it does not have both spouses' names on the account. Taken one step further, the spouse may want to put *the daughter's name on a $10,000 account as the designated beneficiary* so that this account also avoids probate.

Second, if any trust is used (for example, something left to a spouse in a trust set up in a will to avoid estate tax when both spouses have died), then there must be a solely-owned asset to fund the trust. Otherwise, the surviving spouse gets everything through joint ownership, and there is nothing available to fund the trust set up in the will.

Remember our previous discussions (in chapter 18 and again at the beginning of this chapter) on stepped-up basis at time of death: when spouses own property jointly, one-half is treated as belonging to each spouse. The significance of this fact is brought out in my next money-saving suggestion, and is another reason spouses may decide *against* joint ownership.

Sample Situation

The case for anyone, including husbands and wives, owning assets jointly with right of survivorship is to avoid the costs of probate. For many individuals this avoidance of probate costs makes joint ownership desirable. Be aware, however, that joint ownership lessens your control over the asset and may allow creditors of one owner of the asset to tie up the asset. But the case where it is absolutely essential that spouses, or anyone else, do *not* own all their property jointly is where there are testamentary trusts. Once again I stress this rule: if there are testamentary trusts (established to *avoid estate tax* and to determine who *eventually receives the money* when the surviving spouse dies), there must be assets owned solely by the husband and solely by the wife. Otherwise, *there will be no available funds to be held by the trust.*

Money-Saving Suggestions

When a joint owner dies, the Internal Revenue Service presumes that this deceased owner held the *entire* interest in the property (and although this presumption can be rebutted, it is sometimes a difficult task). However, if the joint owners are husband and wife, the law concludes that each owns half of the asset. You saw this example at the outset of this chapter. Let me show you a situation where it might be advantageous from a tax point of view for either a husband or wife to have *sole* ownership of an asset.

Suppose a husband and wife jointly own an asset that has increased in value. *It might be advisable to have the asset solely owned by the spouse with the shorter life expectancy, rather than jointly owned.* This is particularly true if there is the possibility of the asset being sold by the surviving spouse. For example, suppose a sixty-year-old wife and a seventy-seven-year-old husband own a building. They might decide to have the *husband own the property in his name alone.* Upon his death (which actuarily will occur first), if the property is then sold by the widow, no income tax is owed on the sale. The reason for this tax consequence is that any gain upon sale is measured from the value at the time of the owner's death (the stepped-up basis at time of death which we have already discussed in chapter 18).

However, if jointly owned (which is the example at the outset of this chapter), upon the death of the husband, he is considered to have owned only one-half the asset. Therefore, only his half of the asset receives the stepped-up basis. But remember that decisions are based not *only* on taxation considerations. Perhaps one spouse does not want the *other spouse to have sole ownership of the asset.* Most importantly, do not start transferring ownership of assets without discussing with your attorney *all the ramifications of this generalized summary,* particularly if you live in a community property state.

MORE ON ATTORNEYS

There are many books on the subject of inheritance. Most of them have a clear message—*stay away from attorneys.* Form books, "how to avoid probate" books, and books about how inheritances are dissipated through legal fees are constantly being published. The cry is for joint ownership; the clamor is for living trusts.

But here is something that many of the how-to books overlook. The attorney makes money not in writing wills, not in probating wills, and not in giving legal advice to the personal representative of the estate. These fees only pay the attorney's office expenses. The attorney makes the real money—and a substantial amount of it—*when something goes wrong.* The fees earned when a wealthy person dies can be large, because the problems can involve substantial amounts of money. The legal problems are launched by *aggressive heirs* who realize that the affairs of the deceased are in disarray, or the problems are launched by an Internal Revenue Service agent drooling at the possibility of a *substantial tax.*

My point is that the legal fee resulting from following general advice, which may be incomplete or inaccurate for a particular situation, will be substantially higher than the legal fee that would have been charged at the outset.

Sample Situation

Just as sometimes there is resentment toward attorneys who charge a fee because someone dies and assets have to be distributed, there also is resentment toward those who receive the assets of the deceased. I have witnessed this in so many cases. As one person said to me: "It is so unfair that my dullard relative gets all that money."

Some years ago, this idea was expressed in a more scholarly manner in this excerpt from the *Law Review* of the University of California:

> Inherited wealth is bestowed in an arbitrary fashion which may tend to be inefficient, particularly when compared with the distribution of earned wealth. The latter is generally distributed according to the productivity of the earner. . . . In contrast, inheritance does not tend to flow to those who have proven they can efficiently allocate resources into areas valued by the society. Indeed, bequests are frequently made to those in greatest need—the poorer or the less competent. Hence, there is a tendency for inheritance to flow to those least capable of efficiently employing it. . . . Special problems of efficiency arise when a business is inherited, for the incapable head of an inherited business is much more difficult to get rid of than a hired hand who proves himself incompetent. (22 *UCLA Law Review* 903, 916-917, [1975])

Money-Saving Suggestion

Your need for an attorney is in proportion to your net worth; the wealthier you are, the greater your need to see an attorney. Wealth is a vague standard; however, one yardstick is that $600,000 threshold amount that the federal government has established in the estate tax law. Another standard is your degree of concern that whatever money you have—maybe $20,000—goes to *whom you choose, quickly and inexpensively.* But the *peace of mind* you can experience by discussing your affairs with a trusted attorney should be reason enough for you to consider seeking advice.

INVESTING YOUR LEGACY

Often a legacy is received by someone who is not experienced in handling finances, and there is confusion about how to invest it. Though you should consult your bank or investment counselor, one investment I recommend that is both safe and lucrative is United States Treasury Department securities. I recently read that over the last twenty-five years, these securities outperformed stocks, bonds, gold, silver, oil, coins, and stamps. An additional benefit of Treasury securities is that the yield is free of both state and local income tax.

A question often asked is: Which Treasury security should be purchased, the short-term bill, the intermediate-term note, or the long-term bond? It is a difficult question to answer because it requires a prediction as to where interest rates offered to investors are heading. If you predict a higher rate of return in future years, then purchase a short-term Treasury bill. When it expires you can then buy a treasury security that may have a higher rate of return. If you think rates are now relatively high, perhaps the long-term bond is the choice for you. If you are still in doubt, perhaps the intermediate-term, two-year Treasury note is best.

Keep your recently acquired money *out of the stock market.* If you disagree with me, then consider getting into the stock market gradually, and with the advice of a competent broker recommended to you by a trusted and knowledgeable friend. I give the same advice about *real estate—avoid making a big plunge with those legacy dollars.* If you do, make sure you first educate yourself about real estate. Entry into the real estate market can be financially rewarding (particularly in times of inflation), but it must be done slowly and shrewdly.

If you have received a legacy, be cautious when approached by any investment advisors, certified public accountants, certified financial planners, insurance agents, salespeople, stockbrokers, real estate brokers, or any other people who contact you about investments within a year of the person's death. *Perhaps these advisors have learned of your legacy through an obituary or through public records in the courthouse.* This is a difficult and emotional time for you, so it is not a good time to hire new advisors. You are vulnerable to get-rich-quick schemes, particularly if your legacy is laden with guilt. Invest your legacy in United States Treasury Department securities. My runner-up investment is a deposit at your local bank—one insured by the federal government (FDIC). With a United States Treasury Department security or an insured bank account, you avoid the difficult analysis that goes into hiring a financial advisor and then evaluating complicated investment alternatives.

Sample Situation

Tax-exempt bonds issued by municipalities have the benefit of being free of any federal tax. If issued by your state, then they are also free of your state tax. But there are three areas of concern that I pass along to you.

The first is straightforward: make sure your tax-exempt bond is, in fact, tax exempt. *The yield on some bonds issued by municipalities may be taxable.* Be sure to discuss any contemplated purchase of tax-exempt bonds with your tax advisor, and determine whether you will be taxed on any of the income.

The second concern rests with the *safety of the investment.* Bonds issued by municipalities, unlike the Treasury securities, are not guaranteed by the federal government. Essentially, with municipal bonds you are relying on the financial stability of the municipality. Some bonds, however, are insured; but the yield is lower than uninsured bonds of comparable quality.

The third concern lies in the *volatility of the value* of the tax-exempt municipal bonds. Keep this rule in mind: *if interest rates go up, the value of your bond goes down.* Suppose your thirty-year bond, in the face amount of $100,000, yields interest of ten percent. Assume that the interest rate offered to investors increases to fifteen percent. Perhaps as little as $66,666 would be paid for your $100,000 bond. This is because $66,666 would yield interest income of $10,000 from an investment yielding fifteen percent, the same yield from your $100,000 bond. This danger of loss of principal is not so acute if you are going to hold your bond until maturity. However, if you hold the bond until maturity, you earn less on your money (in my example, ten percent rather than fifteen percent) than the investor whose *capital was available for investment in the higher-yielding bond offerings.*

Money-Saving Suggestions

Since no one knows the future, *no one can tell whether today's interest rate is high or low relative to what the unknown future rate will be.* Therefore, I suggest intermediate-term Treasury securities. For those who prefer tax-exempt municipal bonds, I also suggest the intermediate-term bonds.

Another suggestion is that you buy your United States Treasury Department securities directly from any of the twelve Federal Reserve Banks. That way you save the $25 to $50 handling fee charged by many banks and brokerage firms.

LIVING AND DYING

Planning for death is important, and so is understanding money. But ask yourself if you have ever seen an armored truck, laden with money, as part of a funeral procession. I haven't, so I have concluded—like many others before me—you can't take it with you. *The life you live, and hopefully enjoy, is what is most important.*

The generation reaching middle age in the 1990s will have tremendous financial gain from the legacies received from their parents, who were the children of the Depression. But the more valuable legacy we have already received is the example of the lives led by those who are now our elder citizens.

Sample Situations

Robert Louis Stevenson was in poor health the greater part of his life, but everyone knew he was the world's greatest optimist. One day his wife went into his room and saw him cheerfully working on his manuscript. "I suppose you will tell me that it is a glorious day," she said to him. "Yes," he replied, as he looked out at the sunlight streaming through his window, "I refuse to permit a row of medicine bottles to block the horizon."

There is also this story, told by an Alabama attorney, which I read in the *American Bar Association Journal* a couple of years ago. An attorney's mother asked him, "Do you know how to fix it so some other woman won't be able to marry your father for my money after I die?" The attorney explained to his mother the use of trusts, but his mother was not satisfied. The attorney thought long and hard. When he told his mother that he had a solution, her eyes lit up. "Spend it now," the attorney said. My sad sequel to this story is that she will not spend it now. Like so many elderly people today, she will be afraid her money will run out before she dies.

Money-Saving Suggestion

My suggestion to this woman is to consider purchasing a joint and survivor annuity from an insurance company. In return for her principal amount, she receives a monthly check for as long as she lives, and then her husband, if he survives her, receives a monthly check for the rest of his life. This way Dad is protected from "the other woman."

I end this book with a general observation on money. So many people have extreme attitudes on the subject—either being so *thrifty* that life is not enjoyed to the fullest extent possible, or by being so *profligate* that life is one financial crisis after another. *To the big savers,* I commend your discipline, but I suggest that if you can afford something, like that trip always planned but never taken, then spend the money and enjoy it. Remember that even this book has not taught you how to take it with you. *To the big spenders,* I express my amazement at your inventiveness, but I suggest that the pain of the credit card payments offsets the pleasure of the goods and services purchased on optimism.

I hope that this book has enriched your life, perhaps by showing you ways to save money or, more importantly, by helping you solve a few worrisome problems.

Appendices

Appendix A

A Sample Will

Here is a sample will and an accompanying Affidavit of Witnesses to give you an idea of the form and content of these documents. Because laws differ from state to state and because your particular situation is unique, this sample will is set forth as an example only and thus not intended for use, whether in whole or in part, by the reader. Your will should be prepared by an attorney.

I, THOMAS DOE, residing at (address), do hereby make, publish and declare this instrument to be my Last Will and Testament, hereby revoking any and all wills and codicils heretofore made by me.

FIRST: I direct that all my unsecured enforceable debts and funeral expenses, the expenses of my last illness, and the administration expenses of my estate be paid as soon after my death as may be practicable.

SECOND: I give and bequeath my wearing apparel, jewelry, motor vehicles, household furnishings, books, silverware, glassware, works of art and all other personal and household effects, if I own any of such articles at my death, together with all of my interest in all casualty insurance policies insuring such property against any loss or liability, to my wife, JANE DOE, if she survives me or, if she predeceases me, to my only son, THOMAS DOE, JR.

THIRD: All the rest, residue and remainder of my estate, of whatsoever nature and wheresoever situated, which I may own or to which I may in any way be entitled at the time of my death, including any lapsed or renounced legacies or devises, is referred to in this my Will as "my residuary estate" and shall be disposed of as provided in Article FOURTH of this my Will.

FOURTH: I give, devise and bequeath ONE HUNDRED PERCENT (100%) of my residuary estate to my wife, JANE DOE, if she survives me or, if she predeceases me, to my only son, THOMAS DOE, JR. If he has also predeceased me, then my residuary estate is to go to his children, including adopted children, in equal shares. If there are no children, then my residuary estate is to go to my distributees.

FIFTH: A. I hereby nominate, constitute and appoint my wife, JANE DOE, as Executor of this my Will, and my son, THOMAS DOE, JR., as Successor Executor.

B. I expressly direct that no bond or security of any kind shall be required in any jurisdiction to secure the faithful peformance of duties by either my Executor or her successor if he serves.

C. I authorize and empower any fiduciary at any time acting hereunder to resign without leave of court. Any such resignation shall be effective upon delivery of a written instrument of resignation, duly signed and acknowledged, to any other then acting fiduciary or, if none, to the fiduciary named or appointed to serve as a successor.

IN WITNESS WHEREOF, I have hereunto set my hand to this, my Last Will and Testament, on (date), no counterpart hereof having been executed by me.

(legal signature) _____

THOMAS DOE

The foregoing instrument was, on the day of the date thereof, signed, sealed, published and declared by THOMAS DOE, the Testator therein named, as and for his Last Will and Testament, in the presence of us, the undersigned, who at his request and in his presence and in the presence of each other, have hereunto set our names as witnesses.

(The signatures, printed names and addresses of the witnesses appear here.)

Affidavit of Witnesses

STATE OF_____)
) SS.:
COUNTY OF _____)

Each of the undersigned _____, who also acted as supervising attorney, _____, and _____, individually and severally being duly sworn, deposes and says:

The within Will was subscribed in our presence and sight at the end thereof by THOMAS DOE, the within named Testator, on the _____ day of (month), (year), at the Law Offices of (name and address of attorney).

Said Testator at the time of making such subscription declared the instrument so subscribed to be his Last Will and Testament.

Each of the undersigned thereupon signed his or her name as a witness at the end of said Will at the request of said Testator and in his presence and sight and in the presence and sight of each other.

Said Testator was, at the time of so executing said Will, over the age of eighteen years and, in the respective opinions of the undersigned, of sound mind, memory, and understanding and not under any restraint or in any respect incompetent to make a Will.

The Testator, in the respective opinions of the undersigned, could read, write, and converse in the English language and was suffering from no defect of sight, hearing, or speech, or from any other physical or mental impairment, which would affect his capacity to make a valid Will. The Will was executed as a single, original instrument and was not executed in counterparts.

Each of the undersigned was acquainted with said Testator at such time and makes this affidavit at his request.

The within Will was shown to the undersigned at the time this affidavit was made and was examined by each of them as to the signature of said Testator and of the undersigned.

The foregoing instrument was executed by the Testator and witnessed by each of the undersigned affiants under the supervision of the above-named attorney-at-law.

_____

(Witness Signature)

_____

(Witness Signature)

_____

(Witness Signature)

Severally sworn to before me this _____ day of (month), (year).

_____

(signature and official seal)

Notary Public

Appendix B

INTERNAL REVENUE SERVICE CHART OF
MAXIMUM TAX CREDIT FOR STATE DEATH TAXES

From*	To*	Credit = +	%	Of Excess Over
0	$ 40,000	0	0	0
$ 40,000	90,000	0	.8	40,000
90,000	140,000	400	1.6	90,000
140,000	240,000	1,200	2.4	140,000
240,000	440,000	3,600	3.2	240,000
440,000	640,000	10,000	4	440,000
640,000	840,000	18,000	4.8	640,000
840,000	1,040,000	27,600	5.6	840,000
1,040,000	1,540,000	38,800	6.4	1,040,000
1,540,000	2,040,000	70,800	7.2	1,540,000
2,040,000	2,540,000	106,800	8	2,040,000
2,540,000	3,040,000	146,800	8.8	2,540,000
3,040,000	3,540,000	190,800	9.6	3,040,000
3,540,000	4,040,000	238,800	10.4	3,540,000
4,040,000	5,040,000	290,800	11.2	4,040,000
5,040,000	6,040,000	402,800	12	5,040,000
6,040,000	7,040,000	522,800	12.8	6,040,000
7,040,000	8,040,000	650,000	13.6	7,040.000
8,040,000	9,040,000	786,800	14.4	8,040,000
9,040,000	10,040,000	930,800	15.2	9,040,000
10,040,000	. . . .	1,082,800	16	10,040,000

* Adjustable taxable estate amount, which is the decedent's taxable estate less $60,000.

Glossary

Abatement: A proportional reduction of monetary legacies, when the funds or assets out of which such legacies are payable are not sufficient to pay them in full.

Ademption: Extinction of a legacy by a testator's act equivalent to revocation or indicating intention to revoke, i.e., selling or giving away the object during one's lifetime, thus making it unavailable to be distributed at time of death.

Administrator of an estate: A person appointed by a court to administer (i.e., manage or take charge of) the assets and liabilities of a deceased, when such person has died without a will (and therefore without having named an executor).

Advancement (of a legacy): Money or property given to a legatee and intended to be deducted from a legacy stated in the will.

Affidavit(s) of the witness(es): A signed statement made voluntarily by a witness to a will and confirmed by the oath of the witness taken before a notary public. This statement recites the observations of the witness at the time the testator signed the will.

Alimony: Money that a husband or wife by court order pays to the other for maintenance while they are separated or after they are divorced.

Ancillary Letters Testamentary: Authorization by a court, in a state other than where the deceased was domiciled, given to an executor to administer the deceased's real property in this other state.

Ancillary Probate Proceeding: Estate administration in a state, other than the state where decedent was domiciled, where decedent owned real property (land and any structures thereon).

Assets with right of survivorship: An asset having two or more owners, and the survivors among these owners succeed to the deceased owner's interest in the asset.

Basis: Acquisition cost, or some substitute therefor, of an asset, and this basis is used in computing gain or loss on sale of the asset. An example of "some substitute therefor" is the stepped-up basis (or stepped-down basis) which an heir receives for property acquired from a deceased's estate.

Beneficiary: One who benefits from an act of another, such as a beneficiary of a trust or a beneficiary of a will.

Bequeath: To give personal property by will to another. It therefore is distinguishable from "devise," which is a testamentary disposition of real property (land and any structures thereon).

Buy-Sell Agreement: An arrangement, particularly appropriate in the case of a closely held corporation or a partnership, whereby the surviving owner(s) (i.e., shareholders or partners) of the entity (i.e., corporation or partnership), or the entity itself, agree(s) to purchase the interest of a withdrawing or deceased owner (i.e., shareholder or partner).

Charitable Remainder Annuity Trust: A trust that must pay the non-charitable income beneficiary or beneficiaries a certain sum annually, which is not less than a certain percentage (currently 5 percent) of the *initial net fair market value* of all property placed in the trust as valued when the trust is established. Upon the death of the income beneficiary, the charity receives the trust principal.

Charitable Remainder Unitrust: Same as a charitable remainder annuity trust, except the distribution to the income beneficiary is based on the value of the trust as *valued annually*.

Codicil: A separate legal document, signed and witnessed with the same legal formalities of a will, that may explain, modify, add to, subtract from, qualify, alter, restrain or revoke provisions in an existing will. Often simply referred to as an amendment to a will.

Co-executor: One who serves as executor at the same time with one or more other executors.

Common Disaster Clause: See Simultaneous Death Clause.

Conservator: A guardian, protector, or preserver appointed by a court to manage the financial affairs of someone unable to manage his or her financial affairs without some assistance.

Construction proceeding: A court proceeding that interprets an ambiguously worded will.

Creditor: A person to whom a debt is owed by another person (who is called the "debtor").

Death taxes: The generic term to describe all taxes imposed on property or on transfer of property at the death of the owner, including estate and inheritance taxes. See Estate tax; Inheritance tax.

Depreciation: The write-off for tax purposes of the cost, which is subject to certain adjustments, of a tangible (physical) asset over its estimated useful life.

Destroy a will: In relation to wills, the term "destroy" means not only the total physical annihilation of the will into other forms of matter, but a destruction of its legal efficacy, which may be by a written cancellation, obliterating, tearing into fragments, discarding, etc.

Devise: To make a testamentary disposition of land or realty by the last will and testament of the testator.

Disclaimer: The act by which a party refuses to accept an estate, or some part thereof.

Disinherit: The act by which the owner of an estate deprives a person, who would otherwise be his heir, of the right to inherit.

Distributee: An heir; a person entitled to share in the distribution of an estate. This term is used to denote one of the persons who is entitled under the statute of distributions in the state where the deceased was domiciled, to the estate of one who has died intestate (without a will). Also called a next of kin.

Durable Power of Attorney Clause: A clause in a power of attorney document stating that the power remains operative even if the person giving the power becomes mentally incompetent. See Power of Attorney.

Empty nest syndrome: An expression denoting the loneliness parents sometimes feel when their children leave home to pursue their own lives. Opposites are the "return to the nest" or the "never left the nest" syndrome.

Enforceable agreement: An agreement, or contract, that the law recognizes and enforces.

Equitable distribution: Divorce statutes in certain states grant courts the power to distribute equitably, upon divorce, all property legally and beneficially acquired during marriage by husband and wife, or either of them, whether or not legal title lies in the joint or individual names.

Estate: The total property of whatever kind that is owned by a decedent prior to the distribution of that property in accordance with the terms of a will, or, when there is no will, by the laws of inheritance in the state of domicile of the decedent. It means, ordinarily, the whole of the property owned by anyone, the realty as well as the personalty.

Estate tax: A tax imposed on the deceased's estate. Thus, an estate tax is levied on the decedent's estate and not on the heir receiving the property. It is a tax levied on the right to transmit property, while an "inheritance tax" is levied on the right to receive property. See Inheritance tax.

Executor: A person appointed by a testator to carry out the directions and requests in his will, and to dispose of the property according to testamentary provisions after the testator's death.

Executor's commission: A fee the executor receives for administering a deceased's estate.

Generation-Skipping Transfer tax: A tax on the transmission of wealth from older-to-younger generation recipients that would otherwise avoid the transfer tax (estate tax or gift tax) payable by an intervening generation.

Gift tax: A tax imposed on the transfer of property by gift. Such tax is based on the fair market value of the property on the date of the gift. However, under current law gifts of $10,000 or less may be made annually, to an unlimited number of recipients, without incurring a federal gift tax.

Grantor: The creator of a trust is usually designated as the grantor of the trust. See Settlor.

Gross assets of an estate: The property owned or previously transferred by a decedent that will be subject to the federal estate tax. It includes the probate estate, which is property actually subject to administration by the administrator or executor of an estate. It also includes the nonprobate assets of the deceased, such as joint bank accounts and proceeds of life insurance.

Guardian: A person lawfully invested with the authority and charged with the duty of taking care of a person. One who manages the property and rights of another person.

Homestead right: Property set apart by the court for the use of a surviving husband or wife and the minor children out of the commonly owned property or out of the real estate belonging to the deceased.

Inheritance tax: A tax imposed in some states upon *recipients* of estate assets, but close relatives of a deceased are often exempt from this tax.

Insurance: A contract whereby, for a stipulated price, one party undertakes to compensate the other for loss on a specified subject by specified perils.

    Disability insurance: Type of insurance protection purchased to cover payments for a work-precluding injury.

    Homeowner's insurance: Policy insuring individuals against any, some, or all of the risks of loss to personal dwellings, or the contents thereof, or the personal liability pertaining thereto.

    Liability insurance: Insurance that covers suits against the insured for damages such as injury or death to others, or property damage, and the like. It is insurance for those damages for which an automobile driver, for example, can be held liable.

    Life insurance: A contract between the holder of a policy and an insurance company (i.e., the carrier) whereby the carrier agrees, in return for premium payments, to pay a specified sum (i.e., the face value or maturity value of the policy) to the designated beneficiary upon the death of the insured.

    Term insurance: Form of pure life insurance having no cash surrender value and generally furnishing insurance protection for only a specified or limited period (term) of time. Such policies are usually renewable.

    Whole life insurance or **Straight life insurance:** Insurance for which premiums are collected so long as the insured may live and these whole life policies build up cash reserves, whereas term policies do not.

In Terrorem Clause: A clause in a will providing for the revocation of a bequest or devise if the legatee contests the will.

Intestate, (dying intestate): Dying without a will.

Intestate share: The portion of an intestate's estate received by a distributee.

"In Trust For" Account: See Totten Trust.

Joint ownership of assets: An asset with two or more owners, the survivors of whom might succeed to ownership of the deceased's share of the asset, depending upon whether there is the right of survivorship.

Judgment debts: Debts that are evidenced by matter of court or other government agency record. They are debts for the recovery of which judgment has been rendered as the result of a successful legal action.

Legacy: What is received through someone's will.

Legatee(s): The person(s) to whom a legacy in a will is given. The term may be used to denominate those who take under the will without any distinction between land and realty (which is devised) and personalty (which is bequeathed).

Letters of Administration: A formal document issued by a court appointing someone to administer the estate of a person who died without a will.

Letters of Intent: A letter that has no legal enforceability, but merely shows a person's intentions or desires.

Letters Testamentary: The formal instrument of authority and appointment given to an executor by the proper court, empowering him to enter upon the discharge of his office as executor (which is to gather and distribute the assets of the deceased). It corresponds to letters of administration granted to an administrator, appointed when someone dies without a will.

Living (Inter Vivos) Trust: A transfer of property during the life of the owner to a trustee for the benefit of a beneficiary. To be distinguished from a testamentary trust where the property passes at death. (See Testamentary Trust.) Different from a bank account "in trust for" someone, which has no accompanying trust contract. Also different from a Living Will.

Living Will: A document, possessing legal status in most but not all states, signed by an individual stating his or her desires regarding medical treatment in the event of a terminal illness.

Mortgage: An interest in land created by a written instrument providing security for the performance of a duty or the payment of a debt.

Net worth: What remains after deduction of liabilities from assets. Also expressed as the difference between total assets and liabilities of an individual, a corporation, etc.

Nuptial Agreement: See Prenuptial Agreement.

Palimony: Term having a meaning similar to that of "alimony" except that award, settlement, or agreement arises out of the nonmarital relationship of the parties (i.e., nonmarital partners).

Personal effects: Articles associated with a person as property having more or less intimate relation to the person. A broad reference in the context of wills and estate administrations is to the following items owned by a decedent at the time of death: clothing, furniture, jewelry, silverware, china, crystal, cooking utensils, books, cars, televisions, radios, etc. A narrower reference of the term includes only such tangible property as attended the person, or such tangible property as is worn or carried about the person.

Personal property: Everything other than land or realty. See Real property, which is land and buildings.

Personal Representative of the Estate: Term applied to either an executor (when there is a will) or administrator (when there is no will).

Power of Attorney: An instrument authorizing another to act as one's agent or attorney. The agent is attorney in fact and the power is revoked on the death of the principal by operation of law. Such power may be either general or limited. See also Durable Power of Attorney Clause.

> **General Power of Attorney:** Allows another to act in all matters as one's agent.

> **Limited Power of Attorney:** Allows another to act as one's agent in some limited situation(s), such as granting this power to someone to withdraw money from a particular bank account.

Predecease: To die before; the correlative of "succeed."

Preliminary Letters Testamentary: Limited authorization for a person named as executor in a deceased's will to protect the assets of the estate prior to the will being admitted to probate (which results in the issuance of Letters Testamentary).

Prenuptial Agreement: An agreement entered into by prospective spouses prior to marriage but in contemplation and in consideration thereof. By it, the property rights of one or both of the prospective spouses are determined in the event of divorce or death. Called a post-nuptial agreement if entered into during the marriage.

Probate assets: Those assets of the deceased distributed in accordance with the terms of the last will and testament. Property that has a named beneficiary (or jointly owned with right of survivorship) is not probate property.

Probate Court: A court having general powers over probate of wills, administration of estates, and, in some states, empowered to appoint guardians and conservators. A court with similar functions is sometimes called a Surrogate's or Orphan's Court in certain states.

Probate law: The body or system of law relating to all matters of which probate courts have jurisdiction.

Progressive tax rate: A type of graduated tax, as in the case of the federal income tax, which applies higher tax rates as income increases.

Public Administrator: When a person dies without a will (and therefore without an executor), a distributee (or legatee) is appointed to serve as the administrator. If there is no one available to so serve, then a public official of the community serves as administrator. This official is often called the community's public administrator.

Publication: The formal declaration made by a testator at the time of signing a will that it is a last will and testament and the request to witnesses to witness the signing thereof.

QTIP Trust: An abbreviation for Qualified Terminable Interest Property Trust, it is a trust for a spouse's benefit that qualifies for the marital deduction and also allows the spouse establishing the trust to determine the ultimate beneficiary upon the other spouse's death. To qualify for the marital deduction, the trust must distribute all the income to the spouse at least annually, the spouse receiving the income must be a United States citizen, and an election must be made to have this trust treated as a QTIP Trust.

Real property: Land and buildings are real property. The most common example of real property is a person's house. See Personal property, which is everything other than real property.

Renunciation by an executor: The act by which a person abandons a right acquired without transferring it to another. In connection with wills, it is the act of a proposed executor waiving his right to so serve.

Residuary estate: That which remains after debts and expenses of administration and legacies have been satisfied. It consists of all the probate estate that has not been otherwise legally disposed of by the will.

Security interest: A form of interest in property that allows for the property to be sold upon default of the obligation for which the security interest is given. A mortgage is used to grant a security interest in real property (land and real estate). A lien is an agreement between creditor and debtor that grants a security interest in personal property (everything other than real property).

Self-proved Will: A will that contains a notarized affidavit of witnesses.

Settlor: One who creates a trust. Also referred to as a Grantor.

Simultaneous Death Clause: A clause in a will that provides for the disposition of property in the event that there is no evidence as to the priority of time of death of the testator and another. Also referred to as a Common Disaster Clause.

Spouse's Elective Share: The minimum percentage of a deceased's estate, despite the will, that state law mandates must go to the surviving spouse.

Statute of limitations: The period of time in which a legal action must be brought.

Stepped-up Basis: An increase in the income tax basis of property received from an estate to the fair market value at death (or to the alternate valuation, which is the value of the property six months after death).

Successor Executor: An executor who follows or succeeds an earlier executor and who has all the powers of the earlier executor. Wills generally make provisions for appointment of one or more successor executors in the event that the primary executor fails or ceases to act. The major reason for a primary executor to fail to act is that this person has predeceased the testator.

Successor Legatee(s): Alternate person(s) named to receive a legacy in the event the predecessor legatee has predeceased the testator or disclaims the legacy. See Disclaimer.

Successor Residuary Legatee(s): Same as successor legatee(s), except he, she, or they succeed to a residuary share of the estate.

Surviving spouse: The spouse who outlives his/her partner. A term commonly found in statutes dealing with probate, administration of estates, and estate and inheritance taxes.

Survivorship Clause: Survivorship occurs when a person becomes entitled to property by reason of his having survived the death of another person who had an interest in it.

Tangible personal property: Property, such as a chair or automobile, that may be touched or felt. It is in contrast to symbolic property such as a stock certificate that represents ownership of part of a corporation, or a bank account that represents the money in the account, and this symbolic property is intangible personal property.

Taxable estate: The gross estate (all the assets) of a decedent reduced by certain tax deductions, e.g., administration expenses, marital and charitable deductions, etc.

Tax audit: The review and questioning by the government of a tax return.

Tax avoidance: Legally planning your affairs so as to minimize, or avoid, tax.

Tax credit: An actual reduction of tax by the amount of the credit. More valuable than a tax deduction.

Tax deduction: A reduction of the amount to which a tax is applied.

Tax deferral: A legally permissible delay of payment of a tax.

Tax evasion: The crime of not paying tax that is legally owed.

Tax exempt: Free of tax, e.g., the interest income on certain municipal bonds that is not subject to federal income tax.

Tax schedules: A chart showing tax rates.

Testamentary capacity: It is the testator's capacity to know the general nature and extent of property the testator owns and those persons to receive this property at the time of the testator's death. It is a minimum awareness standard required of someone signing a legally enforceable will.

Testamentary Trust: A trust that takes effect at the death of the testator. It is contained within a will. See Living Trust.

Testator: One who makes or has made a will; one who dies leaving a will.

Totten Trust Account: It is created by the deposit by a person of his own money in his own name with a revocable designation of someone who is to receive the amount in the account at the time of the depositor's death. An example of a Totten Trust is a bank account that is owned by John and "in trust for" (i.t.f.) Mary. A "payment on death" (often abbreviated with the capital letters P.O.D.) account is similar.

Trust Agreement: An agreement whereby one person, called a trustee, holds property for the benefit of another, called a beneficiary. See Living Trust; Testamentary Trust.

Trustee: A person holding property for the benefit of a beneficiary in trust. The trustee has the legal title to this property, which is held for the benefit of another.

Valuable Items Rider (to homeowner's insurance policy): A separate insurance agreement, usually associated with a homeowner's insurance policy, whereby items such as jewelry and furs are insured.

Witness to a will: One who has observed the testator signing the will and subscribes his or her own name thereto. Most state statutes require two attesting witnesses, although some states require three such witnesses. In some states the witness is required to witness the other witnesses signing as witnesses.

Index